# CATAPULT

## ENGLISH LANGUAGE

*Adrian Cropper*

*Answers by*
Peter Ellison and Jane Branson

**OXFORD**
UNIVERSITY PRESS

# OXFORD
## UNIVERSITY PRESS

Great Clarendon Street, Oxford, OX2 6DP, United Kingdom

Oxford University Press is a department of the University of Oxford. It furthers the University's objective of excellence in research, scholarship, and education by publishing worldwide. Oxford is a registered trade mark of Oxford University Press in the UK and in certain other countries

British Library Cataloguing in Publication Data

Data available

ISBN 978-0-19-842536-6

10 9 8 7 6 5 4 3 2 1

Printed in Great Britain by CPI Group (UK) Ltd., Croydon CR0 4YY

We are grateful for permission to include extracts from the following copyright material:

**Sean B Carroll**: *The Serengeti Rules: the quest to discover how life works and how it matters* (Princeton University Press, 2017), reprinted by permission of PUP.

**Gillian Clarke**: 'Cold Knap Lake' from *Collected Poems* (Carcanet, 1997), copyright © Gillian Clarke 1997, reprinted by permission of Carcanet Press Ltd.

**Helen Cresswell**: *Moondial* (Faber/Penguin, 1987), copyright © Helen Cresswell 1987, reprinted by permission of Faber Faber Ltd.

**Severn Cullis-Suzuki**: 'I'm Only a Child, but...' speech representing the Environmental Children's Organization at the UN Conference on Environment and Development (1992), reprinted by permission of Severn Cullis-Suzuki.

**Carl Dos Santos**: 'Skydiving' from www.adventureliving.com, reprinted by permission of the author.

**Alan Gibbons**: *The Edge* (Dolphin, 2002), copyright © Alan Gibbons 2002, reprinted by permission of Orion Children's Books, an imprint of Hachette Children's Books, Carmelite House, 50 Victoria Embankment, London, EC4Y 0DZ.

**Guy Grieve**: 'The day I survived a very grizzly bear attack', *Daily Mail*, 26 Nov 2009, reprinted by permission of Solo Syndication/Associated Newspapers Ltd.

**Idaho Public Television**:'Robotics: Facts', Science Trek, Idaho Public Television, (http://www.idahoptv.org/sciencetrek), reprinted by permission of Idaho Public Television.

**The Independent**: Letter to the Editor, 'Please stop treating wheelchair users as if they are invisible', The Independent, 29 Nov 2017, copyright © *The Independent* 2017, reprinted by permission of Independent Print Ltd/ ESI Media.

**Jonathan Jones**: 'A picture of loneliness: you are looking at the last male northern white rhino', *The Guardian*, 12 May 2015, copyright © Guardian News & Media Ltd 2015, reprinted by permission of GNM.

**Rob Lloyd Jones**: *Wild Boy* (Walker Books, 2013), copyright © Robert Lloyd Jones 2013, reprinted by permission of Walker Books Ltd, London SE11 5HJ, www.walker.co.uk

**Gill Lewis**: *White Dolphin* (OUP, 2012), copyright © Gill Lewis 2012, reprinted by permission of Oxford University Press.

**Geraldine McCaughrean**: *Where the World Ends* (Usborne, 2017), copyright © Geraldine McCaughrean 2017, reprinted by permission of David Higham Associates.

**Cara McGoogan**: 'Delivery robots to replace takeaway delivery drivers in London trial' *The Telegraph*, 6 July 2016, copyright © Telegraph Media Group Ltd 2016, reprinted by permission of TMG.

**Patrick Ness**: *More Than This* (Walker Books, 2013), copyright © Patrick Ness 2013, reprinted by permission of Walker Books Ltd, London SE11 5HJ, www.walker.co.uk

**Leslie Norris**: 'The Tiger' from *Leslie Norris: The Complete Poems* (Seren, 2008), reprinted by permission of Professor Meic Stephens.

**Jennifer O'Connor**: '5 Reasons NEVER to buy a snake' from www.peta.org, reprinted by permission of People for the Ethical Treatment of Animals

**Maggie O'Farrell**: *I Am, I Am, I Am: Seventeen brushes with death* (Tinder Press, 2017), copyright © Maggie O'Farrell 2017, reprinted by permission of Headline Publishing Group.

**George Orwell**: 'Shooting an Elephant' first published in *New Writing* 1936, copyright © George Orwell 1936, from *Shooting an Elephant and Other Essays* (Secker & Warburg, 1950), reprinted by permission of A Heath & Co on behalf of Bill Hamilton as the Literary Executor of the Late Sonia Brownell Orwell.

**Playing Out**: website www.playingout.net, reprinted by permission of Playing Out CIC.

**RSPCA**: 'What to consider' (for exotic animals as pets) from Advice and Welfare, www.rspca.org.uk, reprinted by permission of the RSPCA.

**J. R. R. Tolkien**: *The Hobbit* (George Allen & Unwin, 1937/ HarperCollins, 2017), copyright © the J. R. R. Tolkien Estate Ltd 1937, 1965, reprinted by permission of HarperCollins Publishers Ltd.

**Angus Watson**: 'I was a Bully', *The Guardian*, 20 March 2010, copyright © Guardian News & Media Ltd 2010, reprinted by permission of GNM.

**Tim Wynne-Jones**: *A Thief in the House of Memory* (Groundwood, 2006/ Usborne, 2007), copyright © Tim Wynne-Jones 2006, reprinted by permission of Groundwood Books Ltd, Toronto, www.groundwoodbooks. com.

**Malala Yousafzai** with Christina Lamb: *I am Malala: the girl who stood up for education and got shot by the Taliban* (Orion, 2016), copyright © Salarzai Ltd 2013, reprinted by permission of The Orion Publishing Group, London

Although we have made every effort to trace and contact all copyright holders before publication this has not been possible in all cases. If notified, the publisher will rectify any errors or omissions at the earliest opportunity.

## Contents

# *Catapult* introduction

*Catapult* has been written to help students develop the skills, knowledge and confidence needed to make the required progress in English across Key Stage 3, particularly those students who may be below the expected standard in reading and writing at the start of secondary school.

Many students arrive at secondary school with poor vocabulary development and a more limited knowledge of the world, which can prevent them from reading with the level of understanding that they need to succeed. These students are often keen and willing to learn, but their poor comprehension of more demanding texts prevents them from making the progress they need to catch up with their peers.

*Catapult* has been designed to support students by providing them with:

- a wide range of engaging, high-quality texts dealing with some of the most important contemporary issues, adding to their general knowledge
- Sophisticated and useful vocabulary that they can incorporate into their writing straight away
- approaches to enable them to comprehend more complex syntax, especially in nineteenth-century texts.

In *Catapult Student Book 1* and *Workbook 1*, you will find high-quality fiction and non-fiction from the 19th, 20th and 21st centuries, organised into chapters designed to build students' understanding of key aspects of fiction, as well as the range of non-fiction purposes and forms they are expected to study. You will find extracts from classic novels by Charles Dickens and Bram Stoker, as well as texts from acclaimed contemporary authors such as Maggie O'Farrell and Patrick Ness.  In addition, a variety of non-fiction texts, including essays, speeches, newspaper articles, biographies, travel writing and guides, have been carefully selected to interest and engage students.

The tasks and questioning throughout *Catapult* have been designed to help students fully comprehend and make sense of the source texts that they encounter. Some of the texts in the Student Book and Workbook have been chosen to be challenging. However, it is important to be honest with the students: if they're not confident readers, then a Dickens sentence won't make much sense to them; if this is the case, encourage your students to acknowledge this and then show them how to make sense of it.

It is generally the case that students who struggle to read mature texts also find it difficult to write convincingly and at length, so in every chapter of the Student Book, Workbook and Kerboodle there are clear links between reading and writing. Students are encouraged to apply their newly-acquired vocabulary and, using the texts as models, to try out new writing techniques. Short exercises gradually build up until the student is ready to use their newly-learned techniques and vocabulary in a more sustained piece of writing.

*Catapult* has been designed not to patronise students but to be clear about how difficult a piece of reading might be, while giving them the key to unlock its meaning. Consequently, this is often a demanding course, because, if students are to catch up, their progress will need to be rapid; however, *Catapult*'s carefully designed, steady, step-by step approach will help them to get there.

Alongside this expectation of accelerated progress *Catapult* endeavours to give students a sense of purpose and achievement. Students need to feel proud of their growing vocabulary and ability to tackle more sophisticated, demanding reading, as well as their increasing control of written language.

Built around core principles of building vocabulary, developing knowledge and understanding, and improving reading and writing skills, *Catapult* will ensure that these students are fully prepared for their future English studies.

## How to use *Catapult*

*Catapult* has been designed with accessibility and engagement in mind. Every unit of the course takes the same approach to build up familiarity while activities throughout provide an increasing level of challenge.

*Catapult* has been built around four key areas that will give students the breadth of knowledge, the vocabulary and the technical understanding that they need to succeed in English:

- building vocabulary
- developing knowledge and understanding
- improving reading habits
- sustaining writing.

By targeting these key areas, building confidence and improving motivation, *Catapult* will help ensure that students make progress and have the opportunity to fulfil their potential.

## Structure

The structure of *Catapult* is straightforward: chapters one and two focus on key aspects of fiction, such as character, setting, action and atmosphere; chapters three to six focus on key purposes and forms in non-fiction, including explanation, opinion, persuasion, advice, arguments and essays.

Each chapter is designed to support students as they develop their reading and writing skills, with the level of challenge rising as students work through the units in each chapter, as well as increasing progressively throughout the Student Book and Workbook as a whole.

## *Catapult* resources

| Try | Apply | Consolidate |
|---|---|---|
| **Student Books:** students will try out new skills, broaden their knowledge and expand their vocabulary.<br><br>Every unit of the Student Book includes:<br><br>- A source text<br>- A Word power activity<br>- A Knowledge and understanding activity<br>- Either a Reading skills or Writing skills activity<br>- A Check your skills activity<br>- Every chapter finishes with either a Reading or a Writing assessment. | **Kerboodle Digital Book plus Lessons, Resources and Assessment:** students will be able to apply the skills, knowledge and vocabulary they have practised in the Student Book.<br><br>Every unit in Kerboodle includes:<br><br>- An audio recording of the source text from the Student Book<br>- An interactive comprehension quiz<br>- A Word power worksheet<br>- Either a Reading skills or Writing skills worksheet<br>- The Student Books are also available as Kerboodle Digital Books, where the resources can be launched directly from the relevant page. | **Workbooks:** students will consolidate everything they have learned. Every unit of the Student Book has a supporting Workbook unit, ideal for additional practice in class or for homework.<br><br>Every Workbook unit includes:<br><br>- A new source text<br>- A range of Word power, Knowledge and understanding, Reading or Writing skills activities<br>- A Check your skills activity |
| **Plan** | | |

**Teacher Books** include guidance on delivering every unit, bringing together the resources from the Student Book and Kerboodle so that you can easily see how they work alongside each other. There are also short-, medium- and long-term plans, as well as answers for all the activities in the Student Book and Workbook.

**Kerboodle** provides a range of additional resources including spelling, punctuation and grammar interactive quizzes, editable versions of assessments, end-of-year assessments, mark schemes, skills-mapping grids and assessment levels.

# How the resources work

## Learning objectives

Each unit of the Student Book and Workbook begins with the learning objectives to be covered. These are the key skills that have been identified as helping students make the required progress in reading and writing. In some units, these objectives predominantly focus on reading skills, while in other units the objectives are focused on writing skills. However, over the course of a chapter, skills in both reading and writing will be covered. In addition to this, all units include an objective that is focused on building student vocabulary, which will benefit both their reading and their writing.

## Introduction and Ready, Set, Go!

Before reading the source text, a brief introduction in the Student Book links the aspect of fiction or non-fiction in focus to students' own reading experiences. Students are then asked a 'Ready, Set, Go!' question to help contextualise the texts they are about to explore and to guide their reading.

## Source texts

Each chapter of the Student Book and Workbook includes extracts from fiction or non-fiction, including texts from the 19th, 20th and 21st centuries. These high-quality extracts have been chosen to engage students as readers and also to enable them to apply the specific skills that the learning objectives focus on. Definitions are provided at the end of the source text for any difficult vocabulary that may impede understanding. In the Student Book, a word count for the source text is also given to provide students with a sense of achievement as they build their reading stamina.

Audio versions of all the sources texts from the Student Book are included in the Kerboodle LRA, enabling all students to access the texts.

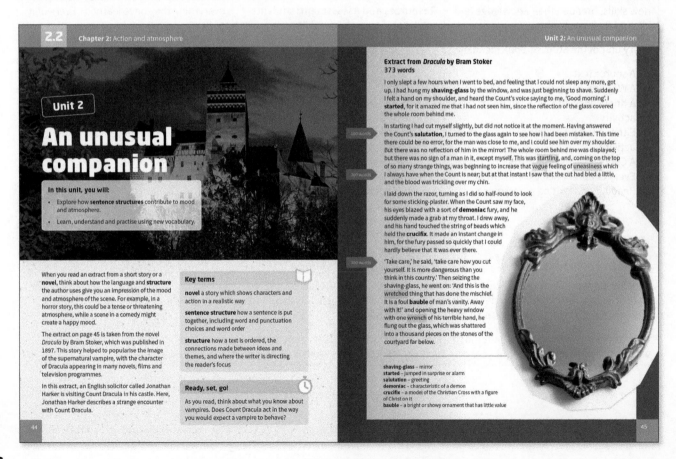

## Word power

At the beginning of the 'Word power' section in the Student Book, students are provided with a list of target vocabulary. These are sophisticated or useful words selected from the source text that will help develop students' understanding of the text's meaning, and also words that students can fruitfully use to improve their own writing. Word power activities in both the Student Book and Workbook help students to understand significant words from the source text or give them the opportunity to use them in their own writing.

Word power worksheets in the Kerboodle LRA further build students' vocabulary and encourage students to practise using the target words from the corresponding Student Book unit.

## Knowledge and understanding

'Knowledge and understanding' questions in the Student Book and Workbook are designed to check student understanding of the source text and develop comprehension skills, moving students from information retrieval to more sophisticated inferential skills.

In addition, there are interactive comprehension quizzes in the Kerboodle LRA linked to every source text in the Student Book, designed to help ensure that students fully understand each text.

## Reading and Writing skills

Depending on the focus of the unit, the questions in this section focus on either reading or writing skills. Reading activities require students to explore language and structural features, developing their critical reading and evaluative skills, as well as providing opportunities for them to share their personal responses to the source text.

Writing activities move students from explorations of specific aspects of writing or writing techniques that are exemplified in the source text (e.g. aspects of grammar and punctuation, structure and organisation, purpose and audience and figurative language techniques) to the articulation of these techniques in their own writing. To appropriately support the development of students' writing skills, these activities move from demanding shorter and more limited responses focused on a single skill or aspect to longer, more extended pieces of writing.

Each unit has an accompanying Reading or Writing skills worksheet on the Kerboodle LRA. These worksheets have been carefully-designed both to support and consolidate the learning in each Student Book unit.

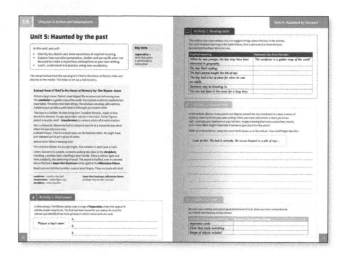

## Check your skills

Each unit in the Student Book and Workbook ends with a more extended activity that is designed to enable students to apply the skills they have developed in the prior section in a more independent context, sometimes asking students to orchestrate a range of skills in their responses.

## End-of-chapter assessment

Each chapter of the Student Book ends with an end-of-chapter assessment. This assessment will have either a reading or a writing focus, and will draw together the skills that students have covered during the chapter. For reading assessments, a new source text is provided followed by the assessment questions, while for writing assessments, a choice of two or three assessment tasks is provided.

## End-of-year assessment

The Kerboodle LRA includes an end-of-year assessment, comprising both reading and writing tasks, along with a number of source texts. Mark schemes and answers will also be provided on Kerboodle, for ease of assessment.

# Getting the most out of the teacher book

## Chapter overview

The chapters in this teacher book link directly to the corresponding student book theme, but also aim to provide you with holistic thematic and practical support, both for planning and lesson delivery purposes. This starts with looking at the 'why', 'what' and 'how' for the chapter as a whole, and then providing a unit sequence designed to boost students' confidence as they progress through the chapter. All of the subsequent ideas and guidance reflect the underpinning philosophy of *Catapult* and provide a suggested route through the student book and digital resources which will help you and your students get the most out of the course.

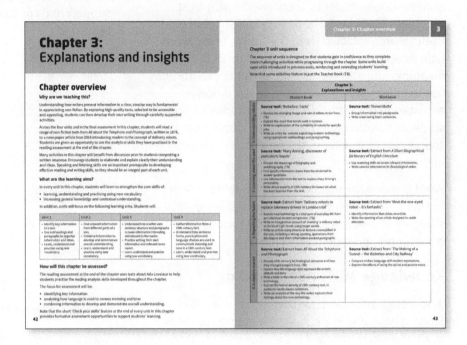

## Preparing to teach

The preparing to teach sections in each chapter aim to equip you with useful background to the theme, saving you time but also enabling you to feel more confident when delivering the unit. Links and wider reading, both for you and your students, are also included. Comprehensive practical teaching tips, in the context of the specific chapter, conclude the preparing to teach section.

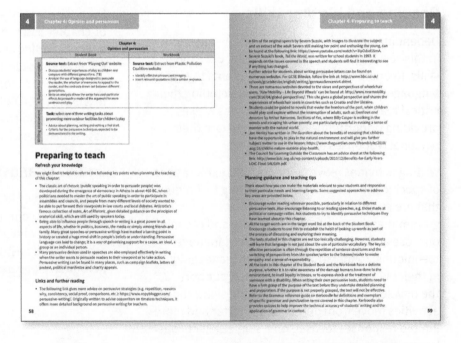

## Unit companions

Each unit in the student book has a corresponding unit companion in this teacher book. The unit companions open with preparation and resources for each specific unit. The main aim of each unit companion is to provide you with guidance on the student book activities and how the Kerboodle resource can be used alongside these. The intention is that they provide you with a teaching sequence to enable your students to develop their skills and build their confidence.

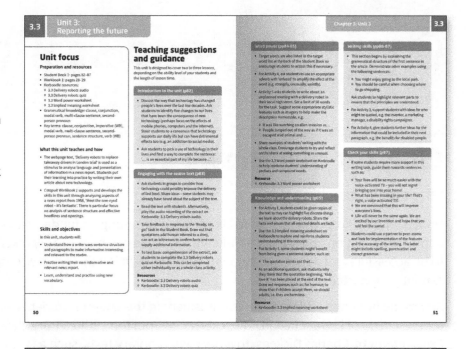

## Assessment suggestions and guidance

Suggestions on how to set up and run the end-of-unit assessments are provided at the end of each chapter, together with guidance on marking. This section also covers how to follow up the assessment and the resources you can use to do this.

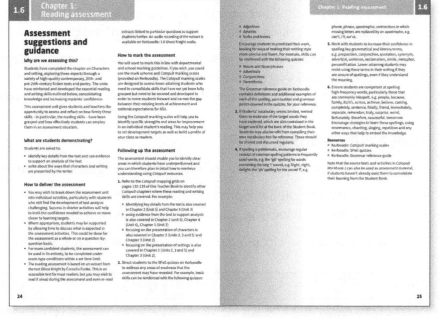

## Answers

Answers to all of the student book and workbook activities are provided in the answers section of this teacher book. There are also answers to reading assessments plus a marking grid for marking both reading and writing assessments is provided on pages 134-137.

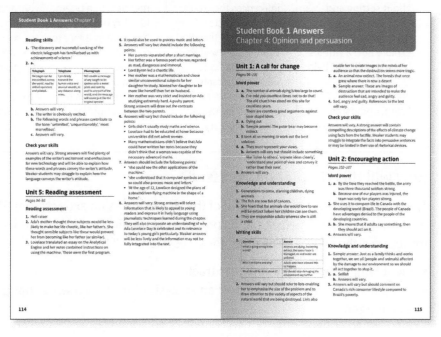

# Chapter 1:
## Characters and setting

## Chapter overview

### Why are we teaching this?

Understanding how writers present characters and settings is fundamental to appreciating fiction and literary non-fiction. By exploring high-quality texts, selected to be accessible and appealing, students can then develop their own writing through carefully supported activities.

Across the five units and in the final assessment in this chapter, students will read a wide variety of literary fiction. The texts range from the 19th-century classic *Great Expectations* by Charles Dickens, to more contemporary texts, such as the novel *White Dolphin* by Gill Lewis. Students are given an opportunity to use the analytical skills they have practised in the reading assessment at the end of the chapter.

Many activities in this chapter will benefit from discussion prior to students completing a written response. Speaking and listening skills are an important prerequisite to developing effective reading and writing skills, so they should be an integral part of each unit.

### What are the learning aims?

In every unit in this chapter, students will learn to strengthen the core skills of:

- learning, understanding and practising using new vocabulary
- increasing general knowledge and contextual understanding.

In addition, the units will focus on the following learning aims. Students will:

| Unit 1 | Unit 2 | Unit 3 | Unit 4 | Unit 5 |
|---|---|---|---|---|
| • Identify key details about setting and characters from a fiction text.<br>• Explore how a writer's language choices help to create a sense of place.<br>• Learn, understand and practise using new vocabulary. | • Develop the inferences they make about characters from the evidence they find.<br>• Explore how writers use flashbacks to develop characters.<br>• Learn, understand and practise using new vocabulary. | • Explore the layers of meaning in a poem.<br>• Identify how the poet has used imagery to reinforce a poem's theme.<br>• Learn, understand and practise using new vocabulary. | • Identify key details and quotations to show understanding of character.<br>• Develop inferences using detailed evidence from the text.<br>• Learn, understand and practise using new vocabulary. | • Read between the lines to find out more about characters.<br>• Explore the words writers choose to describe characters and places.<br>• Learn, understand and practise using new vocabulary. |

### How will this chapter be assessed?

The reading assessment at the end of the chapter uses an extract from *Ghost Knight* by Cornelia Funke to help students practise the reading analysis skills developed throughout the chapter. The focus for assessment will be:

- identifying key details from the extract.
- using textual evidence to support an analysis of the way a writer has presented a character.

Note that the short 'Check your skills' feature at the end of every unit in this chapter provides formative assessment opportunities to support students' learning.

## Chapter 1 unit sequence

The sequence of units is designed so that students gain in confidence as they complete more challenging activities while progressing through the chapter. Some units build upon skills introduced in previous units, reinforcing and extending students' learning.

Note that some activities feature in just the Teacher Book (TB).

| Chapter 1: Characters and setting | | |
|---|---|---|
| | Student Book | Workbook |
| **1: First impressions** | **Source text**: *Skellig* by David Almond<br><br>• Discuss vocabulary focused on a first impression of a person and/or place. (TB)<br>• Analyse a description of place.<br>• Write a description of a deserted school.<br>• Discuss how ideas are drawn from details in the text.<br>• Write an analysis of how the writer creates an impression of character. | **Source text**: *The Hobbit* by J. R. R. Tolkien<br><br>• Identify adjectives that help to build up images of character and setting.<br>• Explore the effects of the writer's word choices. |
| **2: Flashback** | **Source text**: *White Dolphin* by Gill Lewis<br><br>• Discuss happy memories of shared experiences with someone close. (TB)<br>• Analyse homographs in the text.<br>• Explore how the reader gains an impression of character.<br>• Discuss the narrative technique of flashback and the use of past and present tenses.<br>• Write about a childhood memory triggered by a discovery. | **Source text**: *Once* by Maurice Gleitzman<br><br>• Draw inferences from clues in the text.<br>• Analyse a student's writing. |
| **3: Under the surface** | **Source text**: the poem 'Cold Knap Lake' by Gillian Clarke<br><br>• Discuss the unreliability of memory over time. (TB)<br>• Closely analyse language choice.<br>• Analyse possible suggested ideas in the text.<br>• Closely focus on understanding the detail in the poem.<br>• Write a personal response to an opinion expressed about the poem. | **Source text**: the poem 'Adlestrop' by Edward Thomas<br><br>• Explore literal meaning and deeper meaning.<br>• Identify themes. |
| **4: Imprisoned in the past** | **Source text**: *Great Expectations* by Charles Dickens (meeting Miss Havisham)<br><br>• Respond to images of Miss Havisham – discuss reactions and gather vocabulary. (TB)<br>• Write a paragraph about being alone in a strange old house.<br>• Examine the way that the failed wedding affected Miss Havisham, using evidence from the text to support ideas. | **Source text**: *Great Expectations* by Charles Dickens (meeting the escaped prisoner)<br><br>• Identifying an accurate summary.<br>• Understanding what is inferred about a character by descriptive detail. |

| Chapter 1: Characters and setting | | |
|---|---|---|
| | Student Book | Workbook |
| **5: A test of character** | **Source text**: *Where the World Ends* by Geraldine McCaughrean <br><br> • Discuss appropriate vocabulary to describe vulnerability. (TB) <br> • Write a description based on a photograph. <br> • Discuss the writer's use of language in portraying character. <br> • Discuss the use of metaphor in a description of place. <br> • Write an analysis with sentence start support. | **Source text**: *Where The World Ends* by Geraldine McCaughrean <br><br> • Identify a suitable summary. <br> • Write about characters and their relationship. |
| **Reading assessment** | **Source text**: *Ghost Knight* by Cornelia Funke <br><br> • Identify key details from the extract. <br> • Use textual evidence to support an analysis of the way a writer has presented a character. <br> • Use textual evidence to support an analysis of the way a writer has described a place. | |

# Preparing to teach

## Refresh your knowledge

You might find it helpful to refer to the following key points when planning the teaching of this chapter:

- Characters are a vital part of any story; they need to engage the reader's interest whether that is through curiosity, admiration, humour, suspicion, repulsion, horror or simply recognition and empathy. Authors create characters through a variety of means, such as:
  ◇ physical description of their appearance
  ◇ action – what they do
  ◇ what they say
  ◇ what they think and feel
  ◇ what motivates them
  ◇ reaction – how other characters react to them
  ◇ how they change or develop during the story.

- Although there are some classic archetypal characters, such as villains, action heroes and heroines, the most interesting characters are not stereotypes, but more complex. They may embody a mix of virtues and vices, strengths and weaknesses, which means that the reader's attitude towards them is more nuanced and may change as the story progresses. Often, it is the process of discovering or revealing more about the characters that contributes to the story's dynamic and drama.
- The setting of a story is the place and time in which the action takes place. It can be:
  ◇ historical, contemporary or futuristic
  ◇ in a real or fictional location
  ◇ in a specific place, e.g. a school or spaceship
  ◇ at an event, e.g. a holiday or expedition
  ◇ at a particular time of day or time of year.

- The setting may change during a story, often reflecting changes in the plot development and characters' relationships. For example, characters might undergo hardship in winter, find hope in spring, and find resolution and new beginnings in summer.
- Writers often describe the natural world as reflecting the characters' state of mind or emotions. For example, violent storms might accompany a passionate or dramatic encounter between characters. This technique is called pathetic fallacy.

## Links and further reading

- Further information about David Almond, the way he was inspired to write *Skellig* and information about his other work can be found on his website at http://davidalmond.com/. In particular, students could be guided to *My Name is Mina*, which was written as a sequel to *Skellig*.
- Gill Lewis has written extensively about animals and is a vet as well as a writer of
- children's fiction. The following link is her website, which gives further information. about the writer and her works: http://www.gilllewis.com/web/.
- There is information about Gillian Clarke and her work on: http://www.gillianclarke. co.uk/gc2017/. Students could be guided to the poem 'Legend' by Gillian Clarke, which also deals with a memory linked to a lake in childhood.
- There are numerous websites devoted to Charles Dickens and his works. It may be interesting to browse through some of the documents held at the British Library linked to the novel at the following: https://www.bl.uk/romantics-and-victorians/ articles/great-expectations-and-class.
- *Where the World Ends* is reviewed on the following web page: https://www.
- undiscoveredscotland.co.uk/usreviews/books/usbornewhereworldends.html. This
- also links to further information about Warrior Stac and images that can support
- learning. Further information about Geraldine McCaughrean and her writing can be
- found at: https://www.geraldinemccaughrean.co.uk/.
- Cornelia Funke is a prodigious writer and more information about her writing can be found at: http://www.corneliafunke.com/en/buecher. She has written a series called *Ghosthunters*, which will be accessible to all students; some might enjoy *Inkheart* (also a film), which is a more challenging read.

## Planning guidance and teaching tips

Think about how you can make the materials relevant to your students and responsive to their particular needs and learning targets. Some suggested approaches to address key areas are provided below.

- Encourage discussion of students' wider reading wherever possible, particularly in relation to different characters and settings. Draw on their knowledge of any books read earlier in their schooling.
- Draw on students' knowledge of character and setting in relation to other forms, such as film and videogames, and make links between the common techniques used to create these across different forms of fiction.
- All the target words are in the target word list at the back of the Student Book. Encourage students to use this to establish the habit of looking up words as part of the process of discussing and exploring their meaning.
- Students will need more support with the more lexically dense texts. *Great Expectations* is full of rich and evocative vocabulary but preparing some explanations and comparisons ('*It's a bit like…*' ) will help students enormously.
- Refer to the Grammar reference guide on Kerboodle for definitions and exemplars of specific grammar and punctuation terms covered in this chapter. Kerboodle also provides to help improve the technical accuracy of students' writing and the application of grammar in context.

# Unit focus

## Preparation and resources

- Student Book 1: pages 6–11
- Workbook 1: pages 4–5
- Kerboodle resources:
  - ◊ 1.1 Skellig audio
  - ◊ 1.1 Skellig quiz
  - ◊ 1.1 Word power worksheet
  - ◊ 1.1 Setting worksheet
- Grammatical knowledge: adjective, phrase, verb
- Key terms: adjective (WB), alliteration, fiction, novel, phrase, setting, verb

## What this unit teaches and how

- The extract from the novel *Skellig* by David Almond is used as a stimulus to focus attention on the details of characters and settings in a narrative. Later activities explore the way that writers use language to develop a powerful sense of place.

- *Catapult Workbook 1* supports and develops the skills in this unit through an extract from *The Hobbit* by J. R. R. Tolkien, where the reader is introduced to the character Gollum. Students focus on the adjectives used to portray his character and to analyse how the details build up an impression on the reader.

## Skills and objectives

In this unit, students will:

- Identify key details about setting and characters from a fiction text.

- Explore how a writer's language choices help to create a sense of place.

- Learn, understand and practise using new vocabulary.

# Teaching suggestions and guidance

This unit is designed to cover two to three lessons, depending on the ability level of your students and the length of lesson time.

## Introduction to the unit (p6)

- Introduce the unit by asking students when they remember feeling wary and/or suspicious when meeting someone or going somewhere for the first time. (It could be a childhood or a recent experience.)

- Gather vocabulary that describes a sense of suspicion. Students can work in pairs and then share ideas with the whole group. Offer some words to start the activity, e.g. unusual, odd, weird. Tell students that they will use some or all of these words in later writing.

- Alternatively, or in addition, use the 1.1 Setting worksheet on Kerboodle to encourage students to link ideas about settings to different genres.

**Resource**
- ◊ Kerboodle: 1.1 Setting worksheet

## Engaging with the source text (p7)

- If possible, read the source text with the lights low. You could invite a couple of students to mime the characters as the text is read. Ask students if there are any details that place the text in any particular historical time.

- Play the audio recording of the extract on Kerboodle: 1.1 Skellig audio.

- Take feedback on ideas in response to the 'Ready, set, go!' task. Encourage discussion of first impressions of the setting. Draw attention in particular to the description of 'something little and black' scuttling across the floor. Point out the image of the mouse. Do students think this might have been the creature? Encourage speculation and their response to seeing mice running around anywhere.

- To test basic comprehension of the extract, ask students to complete the 1.1 Skellig quiz on Kerboodle. This can be completed as a whole-class activity or individually.

**Resources**
◇ Kerboodle: 1.1 Skellig audio
◇ Kerboodle: 1.1 Skellig quiz

## Word power (pp8-9)

- The writer's use of language is explored through target words and students are then asked to practise creating a sense of place in their own writing. Students could also use the words noted in the introductory activity.

- Use the image and question in the caption to stimulate discussion and ideas before students start their own writing in Activity 6.

- Encourage students to use the 1.1 Word power worksheet on Kerboodle to cement their understanding of the target words, and to develop their knowledge of powerful adjectives that could also be used in their writing task.

- Ask all students to self-assess and be prepared to read their best descriptive sentence from their paragraph.

**Resource**
◇ Kerboodle: 1.1 Word power worksheet

## Knowledge and understanding (p10)

- Draw attention to the image and the question in the caption to stimulate discussion.

- Ask all groups in the class to answer the first question. Then assign different groups across the class to answer one of the subsequent questions in this section.

- After five minutes, share ideas for the first question as a class. Discuss why controlling breathing is a way of relieving stress. Ensure that all students understand and agree on the rest of the answers for this section.

## Reading skills (p11)

- The obvious details are: 'head tipped back', 'covered in dust and webs', 'face was thin and pale', 'black suit', 'closed eyes'.

- Encourage students to explain their ideas as fully as possible, incorporating close references to the text, e.g. 'covered in dust and webs' suggests that he has been there for a very long time and has not moved – this might mean that he is dead.

## Check your skills (p11)

- Students should have access to all the notes made in the previous activity.

- They are asked to write a paragraph, so students will need to expand on the original ideas and use the text references as evidence in support for their ideas. Discuss how to use a variety of verbs to describe what the writer has 'done' to affect the reader, e.g. portrays, illustrates, depicts, etc.

- The following sentence structures could support students' explanations:

  ◇ When the writer describes the figure as…, this suggests that…
  ◇ The words… and… make the reader feel that…
  ◇ The head of the figure is… and this clearly gives the impression that…
  ◇ The contrast between his 'white face' and 'black suit' is used to…

# Unit focus

## Preparation and resources

- Student Book 1: pages 12–17
- Workbook 1: pages 6–7
- Kerboodle resources:
  ◇ 1.2 White Dolphin audio
  ◇ 1.2 White Dolphin quiz
  ◇ 1.2 Word power worksheet
  ◇ 1.2 Appealing to the senses worksheet
- Grammatical knowledge: adjective, noun, past and present tenses, verb
- Key terms: context, flashback, inference, narrator (WB), noun, past tense, present tense, simile, verb (WB)

## What this unit teaches and how

- The extract from the novel *White Dolphin* by Gill Lewis is used to stimulate students' understanding of the way inferences are used by writers to create impressions of character.

- *Catapult Workbook 1* may also be used to support and develop the skills in this lesson through exploring an extract from *Once* by Morris Gleitzman. The extract also blends the past and present, this time from the perspective of an older child. Further activities focus closely on the use of the past and present tenses in the text.

## Skills and objectives

In this unit, students will:

- Develop the inferences they make about characters from the evidence they find.

- Explore how writers use flashbacks to develop characters.

- Learn, understand and practise using new vocabulary.

# Teaching suggestions and guidance

This unit is designed to cover two to three lessons, depending on the ability level of your students and the length of lesson time.

## Introduction to the unit (p12)

The extract from *White Dolphin* touches on the emotional issue of the absence of a family member. Sensitivity about when this unit is taught may be necessary.

- Ask students to think about a memory they have of sharing a happy experience with someone close, e.g. a member of their family or a friend. Ask students to work in pairs to create a diagram describing the feelings they have about this treasured memory. They should focus on the emotions felt rather than descriptive detail of the event.

- Gather feedback on the subject. Collect ideas on the board and encourage students to jot down new ideas/words. Be sensitive about the range of feelings expressed, particularly if some students are recollecting experiences with family members who are no longer with them.

## Engaging with the source text (p13)

- Set the scene for the extract by comparing it to tuning into someone else's thoughts due to the first-person perspective. Kara's reference to her mother in the past tense emphasises her poignant sense of loss. If reading aloud, you should use selective pauses to heighten the emotional impact.

- Play the audio recording of the extract on Kerboodle: 1.2 White Dolphin audio. Compare the way the different readings conveyed the text.

- Draw attention to the 'Ready, set, go!' task. Encourage students to share their first impressions of the character Kara.

- To test basic comprehension of the extract, ask students to complete the 1.2 White Dolphin quiz on Kerboodle. This can be completed as a whole-class activity or individually.

**Resources**
◇ Kerboodle: 1.2 White Dolphin audio
◇ Kerboodle: 1.2 White Dolphin quiz

## Word power (pp14–15)

- The main activity asks students to look at the way particular words make sense in context. Ask students to think of homographs (words with the same spelling but different meaning) outside the text and make a list, e.g. bored, bow, bear, desert, sow, close, lead, wind. Draw attention to how homographs are often different word classes, e.g. noun, verb, adjective, etc.

- Target words are also listed in the target words list at the back of the Student Book so encourage students to access this if necessary.

- For Activity 6, it may help to have a short film clip or image to exemplify the action of the dolphin.

- Use the 1.2 Word power worksheet on Kerboodle to reinforce students' understanding of vocabulary in the extract.

**Resource**
◇ Kerboodle: 1.2 Word power worksheet

## Knowledge and understanding (p16)

- Tell students to work in pairs to consider these activities. All the questions ask students to explore the way that details lead to distinct impressions, e.g. that Kara is daring or patient.

- Ask students to write their answers on sticky notes to be collected. These can be shared anonymously and discussed in a plenary.

- Ask students a further question based on the final part of the text: Why do you think Kara wanted to believe that her mother had sent her a sign? Students may focus on her emotional state and her need to see what she saw.

## Writing skills (p17)

- The focus is on the use of past and present tenses in the flashback technique. In addition to the activities, look at how the conditional can be used to express possibility: would, could, etc.

- Ensure that students understand the terms for imagery: visual (what we see), aural (what we hear), tactile (what we touch), olfactory (what we smell).

- Use the 1.2 Appealing to the senses worksheet on Kerboodle to reinforce students' understanding of the use of the senses when writing about an experience.

**Resource**
◇ Kerboodle: 1.2 Appealing to the senses worksheet

## Check your skills (p17)

- Students are asked to write about finding something that reminds them of a moment from their childhood. Stimulus ideas are suggested but it may be useful to practise planning one idea as a whole class to give support to students who find creative writing particularly difficult.

- Plan ideas on the board and/or draft a few example sentence starters to demonstrate the technique of beginning in the present and moving to the past, e.g.

  ◇ When I see the old brown bear still sitting on my bed, it reminds me of the day that Dad brought it home after queuing for hours…
  ◇ It is hard to understand now that this tatty old children's book once meant so much to me…
  ◇ I walk into the room and instantly feel like the child I was so long ago…

# Unit focus

## Preparation and resources

- Student Book 1: pages 18–23
- Workbook 1: pages 8–9
- Kerboodle resources:
  - ◇ 1.3 Cold Knap Lake audio
  - ◇ 1.3 Cold Knap Lake quiz
  - ◇ 1.3 Word power worksheet
  - ◇ 1.3 Symbolism worksheet
- Grammatical knowledge: adjective, adverb, verb
- Key terms: adjective, adverb, imagery, literal meaning (WB), rhyming couplet, stanza, symbol

## What this unit teaches and how

- The poem 'Cold Knap Lake' by Gillian Clarke is used to help students explore the way that the writer has offered more than a surface meaning about a childhood memory.

- *Catapult Workbook 1* may also be used to support and develop the skills in this lesson through looking at the poem 'Adlestrop' by Edward Thomas. The activities move from ensuring understanding of the literal to exploring other possible themes.

## Skills and objectives

In this unit, students will:

- Explore the layers of meaning in a poem.

- Identify how the poet has used imagery to reinforce a poem's theme.

- Learn, understand and practise using new vocabulary.

# Teaching suggestions and guidance

This unit is designed to cover two to three lessons, depending on the ability level of your students and the length of lesson time.

## Introduction to the unit (p18)

- Play a brief memory game by displaying a tray of objects for a limited time, then take it away and ask students (working in pairs) to recall and note down exactly what was on the tray. This game should illustrate the unreliability of memory.

- Discuss why memory may play tricks. Draw out that it may protect us from reality, justify our actions, or present a more positive image of us or our family or friends.

## Engaging with the source text (p19)

- Explain that the poem is unusual in that the poet is questioning her own version of events. Ask students to read it quietly to themselves, then ask them what they think the poem is describing.

- Play the audio recording of the extract on Kerboodle: 1.3 Cold Knap Lake audio.

- Draw attention to the 'Ready, set, go!' task. Take feedback from students. They may link the description of the girl as 'blue-lipped' and 'dead' to the word 'Cold' in the title. The image of the girl temporarily 'asleep' before she is revived may link to the word 'Knap' in the title, as it has echoes of a nap (short sleep).

- To test basic comprehension of the poem, ask students to complete the 1.3 Cold Knap Lake quiz on Kerboodle. This can be completed as a whole-class activity or individually.

### Resources
- ◇ Kerboodle: 1.3 Cold Knap Lake audio
- ◇ Kerboodle: 1.3 Cold Knap Lake quiz

## Word power (pp20–21)

- Target words are also listed in the target word list at the back of the Student Book so encourage students to access this if necessary.

- For Activity 1, looking at the reason for the crowd's silence, use the following sentence starters to help students:

  ◇ The crowd is standing silent because…
  ◇ There is a silence because…
  ◇ Nobody wants to speak because…

- To support students' answers to Activity 2, discuss the contemporary use of 'bleating' to mean complaining or moaning about something.

- Use a time-lapse film of a blooming flower to trigger ideas for answers to Activity 4.

- Use the 1.3 Word power worksheet on Kerboodle for further exploration of the effects created by the poet's vocabulary.

**Resource**
◇ Kerboodle: 1.3 Word power worksheet

## Knowledge and understanding (p22)

- For Activity 2, ensure students have the terminology to describe what the mother literally does for the child, i.e. resuscitation, giving the 'kiss of life'.

- Activity 3 may require discussion. It may be difficult for some students to understand why a child would be beaten after nearly dying so explore issues of anxiety and social embarrassment. Discuss students' responses to Activity 3b and encourage them to justify their choices using evidence from the text.

## Reading skills (p23)

- Activity 1 looks at the imagery describing the surface of the lake. Draw attention to the word 'cloudiness' and its implication of things being unclear, moving and transitory. Focus too on the image of swans' feet stirring up the water into uneven, irregular patterns.

- Activity 2 should lead students from the imagery used to describe the lake to what it suggests about the poet's memory. Ensure they understand that the lake could be a symbol of the poet's memory. Ask them whether they get the impression of the lake / poet's memory as clear, steady and strong or changeable and hazy. Support students by guiding them to the line at the start of stanza 4, 'Was I there?'

- Use the 1.3 Symbolism worksheet on Kerboodle to reinforce students' understanding of symbols.

**Resource**
◇ Kerboodle: 1.3 Symbolism worksheet

## Check your skills (p23)

- Ask students to work in pairs to write down lines in the poem in different colours to signify evidence that may support the statement, or not. Some may feel that the same words could be used in different ways.

- Support students in writing their responses, reminding them to use short integrated quotations to support their ideas and to explain their thoughts carefully using phrases such as: this shows…, this suggests…, this portrays….

# Unit focus

## Preparation and resources

- Student Book 1: pages 24–29
- Workbook 1: pages 10–11
- Kerboodle resources:
  ◇ 1.4 Great Expectations audio
  ◇ 1.4 Great Expectations quiz
  ◇ 1.4 Word power worksheet
  ◇ 1.4 Character worksheet
- Grammatical knowledge: adjective
- Key terms: infer, narrator, summary (WB), synonym

## What this unit teaches and how

- The extract from *Great Expectations* by Charles Dickens is the famous scene where Pip is confronted by Miss Havisham for the first time. The activities focus on the detail of the description, what is stated and what can be inferred about the character.

- *Catapult Workbook 1* supports and develops the skills in this lesson through an extract from the same text (Pip's meeting in Chapter 1 with the convict Magwitch). There is further practice in analysing the way Dickens portrays character through looking at what can be inferred from short text extracts.

## Skills and objectives

In this unit, students will:

- Identify key details and quotations to show understanding of character.

- Develop inferences using detailed evidence from the text.

- Learn, understand and practise using new vocabulary.

# Teaching suggestions and guidance

This unit is designed to cover two to three lessons, depending on the ability level of your students and the length of lesson time.

## Introduction to the unit (p24)

- Explain that *Great Expectations* is a novel about the life of a poor orphan boy, Pip, whose 'expectations' in life are suddenly lifted by an unknown benefactor, enabling him to become an educated young gentleman. The source text is from an early scene in the novel when Pip is summoned to visit a strange lady of great wealth.

- Display a series of images of Miss Havisham in her room. They could be drawn from the early illustrations or from the screen and stage productions. Ask students to create a spider diagram of words and phrases evoked by the images.

- Collect the words and phrases in response to the images and discuss what themes are common, e.g. ghostly, frightening, decay. These ideas may help later when writing about the extract.

## Engaging with the source text (p25)

- Remind students of Unit 1 in Chapter 1 where David Almond wrote about the discovery of Skellig. Compare this scene with the first-meeting aspect of the scene in *Skellig* from Chapter 1 – do they describe a young person's feelings in a similar way?

- Play the audio recording of the extract on Kerboodle: 1.4 Great Expectations audio.

- Take feedback on students' response to the 'Ready, set, go!' task. Invite speculation, encouraging students to refer to clues in the text.

- To test basic comprehension of the extract, ask students to complete the 1.4 Great Expectations quiz on Kerboodle. This can be completed as a whole-class activity or individually.

**Resources**
- ◇ Kerboodle: 1.4 Great Expectations audio
- ◇ Kerboodle: 1.4 Great Expectations quiz

## Word power (pp26–27)

- For Activity 1, invite other synonyms for the target words. For example, alternative synonyms for 'lustre' might be sparkle, glow, shimmer.

- Use the 1.4 Word power worksheet on Kerboodle for further exploration of synonyms and effective adjectives.

- The focus on 'took note' in Activity 3 helps students see themselves as observers. The question about what is 'important' is based on the idea that time has frozen. Develop the idea of 'time stood still', relating it to the way Miss Havisham is dressed.

- For Activity 4, offer some of the following ideas which could be included in students' writing:

  - ◇ a coat with a torn sleeve hanging up on a hook…
  - ◇ half a cup of tea left on the table…
  - ◇ a half-burned letter in the fire grate…
  - ◇ one shoe under a chairw…

**Resource**
- ◇ Kerboodle: 1.4 Word power worksheet

## Knowledge and understanding (p28)

- Ask students to work in pairs on the questions in this section. For Activity 1, suggest 'withered bride' to get students started.

- For Activity 2, suggest that students consider her emotional state as well as her physical appearance.

## Reading skills (p29)

- For Activities 1 and 2, refer the students back to some of the words they gathered about their first impressions of Miss Havisham. This should help them to focus on how the writer's choice of words has created an impression of Miss Havisham for them as readers.

- Further questions ask for justification of ideas with textual evidence. Revise how to use short integrated quotations in a way that supports ideas effectively, e.g. 'We know that Pip was frightened as he compared her to a "ghastly waxwork" which had scared him when younger'.

- Use the 1.4 Character worksheet on Kerboodle with students to explore another extract in which the writer embeds clues about a character within the description.

**Resource**
- ◇ Kerboodle: 1.4 Character worksheet

## Check your skills (p29)

- Advise students to use some of the vocabulary gathered earlier to help express their personal reactions to the portrayal of Miss Havisham.

- Model for students how impressions can be explained using certain sentence structures. For example:

  - ◇ Still wearing 'a long white veil' which was 'half arranged' shows that she has…
  - ◇ The untidiness of the room, e.g. the 'half-packed trunks' shows that Miss Havisham could not recover from…
  - ◇ The dramatic way in which Miss Havisham says 'Broken!' makes the reader feel…

# Unit focus

## Preparation and resources

- Student Book 1: pages 30–35
- Workbook 1: pages 12–13
- Kerboodle resources:
  - ◇ 1.5 Where the World Ends audio
  - ◇ 1.5 Where the World Ends quiz
  - ◇ 1.5 Word power worksheet
  - ◇ 1.5 Commenting on similes worksheet
- Grammatical knowledge: verbs
- Key term: metaphor

## What this unit teaches and how

- The extract from the text *Where the World Ends* by Geraldine McCaughrean is used as a stimulus for developing the skills of reading between the lines and exploring vocabulary and language choices.

- *Catapult Workbook 1* supports and develops the skills covered in this unit, through an extract from the same text, with activities about understanding the main point, focusing on an important character and applying reading skills through writing extended responses.

## Skills and objectives

In this unit, students will:

- Read between the lines to find out more about characters.

- Explore the words writers choose to describe characters and places.

- Learn, understand and practise using new vocabulary.

# Teaching suggestions and guidance

This unit is designed to cover two to three lessons, depending on the ability level of your students and the length of lesson time.

## Introduction to the unit (p30)

- Introduce the unit by asking students to work in pairs to discuss what it feels like to be in a small open boat in a choppy sea. This will be mostly imagined, so some guidance may be necessary. If available, you could show a short video clip of a treacherous sea journey.

- Ask students to gather words related to their paired discussion, e.g. violent, unsafe, frightening, scary, worried, etc.

- Gather the thoughts of the groups and start to develop a consensus about the feeling of vulnerability of a young person placed in this position. You could play a loud recording of crashing waves in a storm to emphasise the point.

## Engaging with the source text (p31)

- Ask students to focus on the sea experience that they have just been discussing and the historical context of the source text. You may ask them to consider what safety features of a modern boat would be missing in the 18th century (the time at which the source text is set).

- Take feedback from the 'Ready, set, go!' task about the title of the unit. Draw out how the sea voyage and the prospect of being away from home and in some danger will 'test' the courage and independence of the boys.

- Play the audio recording of the extract on Kerboodle: 1.5 Where the World Ends audio.

- To test basic comprehension, ask students to complete the 1.5 Where the World Ends quiz on Kerboodle. This can be completed as a whole-class activity or individually.

### Resources
- ◇ Kerboodle: 1.5 Where the World Ends audio
- ◇ Kerboodle: 1.5 Where the World Ends quiz

## Word power (pp32-33)

- Activity 5 challenges the students to develop their own writing through careful and appropriate use of the learned vocabulary to describe the photograph of climbers on a steep snow-covered slope. Give students five minutes to complete this activity and set a word limit of 100 words.

- Before they begin, encourage students to use 1.5 Word power worksheet on Kerboodle to explore how to use vocabulary to create emotion or drama in their writing.

- Ask students to read back their paragraphs in groups of four, checking their use of the vocabulary and selecting some 'favourite bits' from across the group. Share these as a class.

**Resources**
◊ Kerboodle: 1.5 Word power worksheet

## Knowledge and understanding (p34)

- Select groups of four to consider the 'Knowledge and understanding' questions on page 34.

- After three minutes, allow one member of each group to visit another group to share answers and then return to their own group to give feedback.

- Share the answers with the rest of the class. Discuss why some answers may have initially been wrong.

## Reading skills (p35)

- Ask students to work in pairs to complete Activity 1. There should be a consensus that one of 'stormy', 'choppy' or 'rough' is the most appropriate – but which one – and why? Students need to be encouraged to explain as carefully as they can in order to emphasise the learning about language choices and the effect on the reader.

- In Activity 2, students can be supported in writing their responses by offering some sentence starters, which include using short references, e.g.

  ◊ Davie is described as 'little', which makes him seem more vulnerable. This is shown when…
  ◊ When Quill thinks 'And bless him', this shows that…

- For Activity 3, direct students to key words from the source text that refer to the size and shape of Warrior Stac, such as 'rock', 'whale', 'pitching', 'whole' and 'bulk'. Use 1.5 Commenting on similes worksheet on Kerboodle to support this task.

- Take feedback from the class and gather students' key impressions of the Stac on the board. Use this as support during the extended writing. You could also include verbs to describe what the writer has 'done' with the image such as: 'portrays', 'illustrates', 'depicts', etc.

**Resources**
◊ Kerboodle: 1.5 Commenting on similes worksheet

## Check your skills (p35)

- Where necessary, provide students with sentence starters to support their writing, e.g.

  ◊ The image is memorable because the writer has used language that makes Warrior Stac seem like a creature, for instance…
  ◊ The reader is made to feel that Warrior Stac is almost alive because…
  ◊ The size and shape of Warrior Stac are emphasised through the use of metaphor…
  ◊ The metaphor… helps the reader to feel… because…
  ◊ We can understand the feelings of the boys in the boat because…
  ◊ The writer's use of 'grows bigger' and 'pushing' helps to…

# Assessment suggestions and guidance

## Why are we assessing this?

Students have completed the chapter on Characters and setting, exploring these aspects through a variety of high-quality contemporary, 20th- and pre-20th-century fiction texts and poetry. The units have reinforced and developed the essential reading and writing skills outlined below, consolidating knowledge and increasing students' confidence.

This assessment unit gives students and teachers the opportunity to assess and reflect on how firmly these skills – in particular, the reading skills – have been grasped and how effectively students can employ them in an assessment situation.

## What are students demonstrating?

Students are asked to:

- identify key details from the text and use evidence to support an analysis of the text
- write about the ways that characters and setting are presented by the writer.

## How to deliver the assessment

- You may wish to break down the assessment unit into individual activities, particularly with students who still find the development of text analysis challenging. Success in shorter activities will help to instil the confidence needed to achieve or move closer to learning targets.
- Where appropriate, students may be supported by allowing time to discuss what is expected in the assessment activities. This could be done for the assessment as a whole or on a question-by-question basis.
- For more confident students, the assessment can be used in its entirety, to be completed under exam-type conditions within a set time limit.
- The reading assessment is based on an extract from the text *Ghost Knight* by Cornelia Funke. This is an accessible text for most readers, but you may wish to read it aloud during the assessment and even re-read

extracts linked to particular questions to support students further. An audio recording of the extract is available on Kerboodle: 1.6 Ghost Knight audio.

## How to mark the assessment

You will want to mark this in line with departmental and school marking guidelines. If you wish, you could use the mark scheme and *Catapult* marking scales (provided on Kerboodle). The *Catapult* marking scales are designed to assess lower-attaining students who need to consolidate skills that have not yet been fully grasped but need to be secured and developed in order to move students forward and narrow the gap between their existing levels of achievement and national expectations for KS3.

Using the *Catapult* marking scales will help you to identify specific strengths and areas for improvement in an individual student's reading. This may help you to set development targets as well as build a profile of your class as readers.

## Following up the assessment

The assessment should enable you to identify clear areas in which students have underperformed and you can therefore plan in detail how to reinforce understanding using *Catapult* resources.

1. Refer to the *Catapult* mapping grids on pages 132-135 of this Teacher Book to identify other *Catapult* chapters where these reading and writing skills are covered. For example:

   ◊ identifying key details from the text is also covered in Chapter 2 (Unit 5) and Chapter 5 (Unit 3)
   ◊ using evidence from the text to support analysis is also covered in Chapter 2 (unit 5), Chapter 4 (Unit 4), Chapter 5 (Unit 2)
   ◊ focusing on the presentation of characters is also covered in Chapter 2 (Units 2, 3 and 5) and Chapter 3 (Unit 2)
   ◊ focusing on the presentation of settings is also covered in Chapter 2 (Units 2, 3 and 5) and Chapter 3 (Unit 2).

2. Direct students to the SPaG quizzes on Kerboodle to address any areas of weakness that the assessment may have revealed. For example, basic skills can be reinforced with the following quizzes:

◇ Adjectives

◇ Adverbs

◇ Verbs and tenses.

Encourage students to proofread their work, looking for ways of making their writing style more concise and fluent. For example, skills can be reinforced with the following quizzes:

◇ Nouns and Noun phrases

◇ Adverbials

◇ Conjunctions

◇ Parenthesis.

The Grammar reference guide on Kerboodle contains definitions and additional examples of each of the spelling, punctuation and grammar points covered in the quizzes, for your reference.

3. If students' vocabulary seems limited, remind them to make use of the target words they have explored, which are also contained in the target word list at the back of the Student Book. Students may also benefit from compiling their own vocabulary lists for reference. These should be shared and discussed regularly.

4. If spelling is problematic, encourage regular revision of common spelling patterns in frequently used words, e.g. the 'igh' spelling for words containing the long 'i' sound, e.g. fright, night, delight; the 'ph' spelling for the sound 'f', e.g.

phone, phrase, apostrophe; contractions in which missing letters are replaced by an apostrophe, e.g. can't, I'll, we've.

5. Work with students to increase their confidence in spelling key grammatical and literary terms, e.g. preposition, conjunction, quotation, synonym, adverbial, sentence, exclamation, simile, metaphor, personification. Lower-attaining students may resist using these terms in their writing if they are unsure of spellings, even if they understand the meaning.

6. Ensure students are competent at spelling high-frequency words, particularly those that are commonly misspelt, e.g. people, because, family, its/it's, across, achieve, believe, coming, completely, sentence, finally, friend, immediately, separate, remember, truly, surprise, weird, fortunately, therefore, successful, tomorrow. Encourage strategies to learn these spellings, using mnemonics, chanting, singing, repetition and any other ways that help to embed the knowledge.

**Resources**

◇ Kerboodle: *Catapult* marking scales

◇ Kerboodle: SPaG quizzes

◇ Kerboodle: Grammar reference guide

Note that the source texts and activities in *Catapult Workbook 1* can also be used as assessment material, if students haven't already used them to consolidate their learning from the Student Book.

# Chapter 2:
## Action and atmosphere

## Chapter overview

### Why are we teaching this?

Understanding how writers present action and create atmosphere is an important part of appreciating fiction. By exploring high-quality texts, selected to be accessible and appealing, students can then develop their own writing through carefully supported activities.

Across the five units in this chapter, students will read a wide variety of fiction. The texts range from the 19th-century novel, *Dracula* by Bram Stoker, to the award-winning 21st-century novel, *A Monster Calls* by Patrick Ness. Students are given the opportunity to use the skills and techniques they have studied in these extracts in the writing assessment at the end of the chapter.

Many activities in this chapter will benefit from discussion prior to students completing a written response. Encourage students to elaborate and explain clearly their understanding and ideas. Speaking and listening skills are an important prerequisite to developing effective reading and writing skills, so they should be an integral part of each unit.

### What are the learning aims?

In every unit in this chapter, students will learn to strengthen the core skills of:

- learning, understanding and practising using new vocabulary
- increasing general knowledge and contextual understanding.

In addition, units will focus on the following learning aims. Students will:

| Unit 1 | Unit 2 | Unit 3 | Unit 4 | Unit 5 |
|---|---|---|---|---|
| • Explore how a writer creates an effective story opening.<br>• Practise building suspense and creating a tense atmosphere in their own writing.<br>• Learn, understand and practise using new vocabulary. | • Explore how sentence structures contribute to mood and atmosphere.<br>• Learn, understand and practise using new vocabulary. | • Explore how a writer describes a dramatic event through description.<br>• Use alliteration and other techniques to create an effective description of a character.<br>• Learn, understand and practise using new vocabulary. | • Identify how the sequencing of events can build suspense.<br>• Explore how an extended metaphor and other techniques can be used to build suspense.<br>• Learn, understand and practise using new vocabulary. | • Identify key details and show awareness of implied meaning.<br>• Explore how narrative perspective, similes and personification can be used to create a mysterious atmosphere in their own writing.<br>• Learn, understand and practise using new vocabulary. |

### How will this chapter be assessed?

The writing assessment at the end of the chapter gives students three different tasks for writing based on the skills practised through the units. There is clear guidance for planning with suggested criteria for inclusion in each piece.

The focuses for assessment will be:

- building suspense and creating a tense atmosphere
- using alliteration and other techniques to describe a character

- describing a sequence of events that suggests excitement and suspense
- using similes, metaphors and personification to create a mysterious atmosphere
- using a wide vocabulary, including some target words from the chapter.

These focuses for assessment may vary in emphasis depending on the writing task that students complete.

Note that the short 'Check your skills' feature at the end of every unit in this chapter provides formative assessment opportunities to support students' learning.

## Chapter 2 unit sequence

The sequence of units is designed so that students gain in confidence as they complete more challenging activities while progressing through the chapter.

Note that some activities feature in just the Teacher Book (TB).

<table>
<tr><td colspan="3" align="center">**Chapter 2:**<br>**Action and atmosphere**</td></tr>
<tr><td></td><td align="center">Student Book</td><td align="center">Workbook</td></tr>
<tr>
<td>**1: A dramatic opening**</td>
<td>**Source text:** *A Monster Calls* by Patrick Ness<br><br>• Discuss the power of dreams and the idea that they are caused by anxiety. (TB)<br>• Analyse language use in the extract.<br>• Track levels of suspense on a graph.<br>• Explore the effect of imagery in conveying a character's tension.<br>• Write an effective next paragraph for the narrative, maintaining the atmosphere.</td>
<td>**Source text:** *The Edge* by Alan Gibbons<br><br>• Assess the effectiveness of the author's use of language to create tension.<br>• Rewrite a story opening to increase its tension and suspense.</td>
</tr>
<tr>
<td>**2: An unusual companion**</td>
<td>**Source text:** *Dracula* by Bram Stoker<br><br>• Explore what is known about vampires. (TB)<br>• Analyse closely archaic and more complex vocabulary.<br>• Focus closely on understanding the detail in the extract.<br>• Analyse grammatically a multi-clause sentence.<br>• Write a continuation of the first-person narrative of the source text.</td>
<td>**Source text:** *The Woman in Black* by Susan Hill<br><br>• Analyse the effect of different sentence types.<br>• Write a continuation of the narrative.</td>
</tr>
<tr>
<td>**3: An awesome stranger**</td>
<td>**Source text:** *Gawain and the Green Knight*, retold by Michael Morpurgo (the arrival of the Green Knight)<br><br>• Discuss Arthurian legend and the concept of knighthood – collect ideas and vocabulary. (TB)<br>• Analyse language use in the extract.<br>• Explore the effects of alliteration.<br>• Write a paragraph that continues the narrative using specific criteria.</td>
<td>**Source text:** *Beowulf*, retold by Michael Morpurgo (the arrival of Beowulf in Denmark)<br><br>• Explore the effects of alliteration in description.<br>• Write a description of Beowulf's face.</td>
</tr>
<tr>
<td>**4: Hidden**</td>
<td>**Source text:** *Moonfleet* by J. Meade Falkner<br><br>• Discuss experiences of feeling trapped in a situation or obliged to keep a promise. (TB)<br>• Analyse closely the use of language to create tension and suspense.<br>• Write a paragraph that explores a dilemma.<br>• Explore the use of extended metaphor.<br>• Analyse the way the writer builds tension and suspense in the text.</td>
<td>**Source text:** *Wild Boy* by Rob Lloyd Jones<br><br>• Explore the use of extended metaphor to create a vivid image.<br>• Sequence events to maximise suspense in a plot.</td>
</tr>
</table>

<table>
<tr><td colspan="3" align="center">Chapter 2:<br>Action and atmosphere</td></tr>
<tr><td></td><td align="center">Student Book</td><td align="center">Workbook</td></tr>
<tr><td rowspan="1">5: Haunted by the past</td><td>Source text: Moondial by Helen Cresswell<br><br>• Discuss and recount experiences that could not be explained at the time. (TB)<br>• Link the style of oral storytelling to the text. (TB)<br>• Focus on second-person narrative and descriptions that appeal to the senses.<br>• Write a continuation of the source text using features explored above.</td><td>Source text: A Thief in the House of Memory by Tim Wynne-Jones<br><br>• Explore implied meanings in the text.<br>• Write a description of a room, giving clues as to events and characters.</td></tr>
<tr><td>Writing assesment</td><td>Task: select one of three creative writing options, all of which demonstrate skills learned through the units<br><br>• Advice about planning and writing a first draft.<br>• Suggestions about tone, style and the intended effect on a reader.<br>• Criteria for the literary techniques to be demonstrated in the writing.</td><td></td></tr>
</table>

# Preparing to teach

## Refresh your knowledge

You might find it helpful to refer to the following key points when planning the teaching of this chapter.

- The action of a story is the events in the plot that drive the story forwards, building on what has gone before, following a sequence of cause and effect, linking different episodes in the narrative. Action in a story should never be for its own sake, but should trigger other events, or reveal something significant about the characters or the situation they are in.
- As the action propels the story forward, tension is built up for the reader. This tension is linked to the reader's curiosity and desire to have their questions answered. The withholding of information, the planting of seeds of suspicion, hints of horror or a sense of impending danger or violence are all techniques used by writers to heighten suspense for the reader. This tension can give a narrative energy and dynamism, ensuring readers will want to read on.
- The atmosphere of a story can be built up through various techniques, e.g. through the description of setting, the characters' feelings and perceptions, their predicament or dilemmas, descriptive language and imagery.
- The narrative voice can also play a key role in creating a specific atmosphere and tone in a story. For example, a first-person narrative (using the pronouns 'I' and 'we') relates events from a single viewpoint; a second-person narrative (using the pronoun 'you') creates a sense of immediacy for the reader, who is deliberately and directly involved in the action of the story; a third-person narrative (using the pronouns 'he', 'she', 'they') is more distant but may be 'omniscient' – able to reveal what is going on inside the heads of all the characters, not just one. Some stories have multiple first-person narrators, switching viewpoints at different times during the action, giving the reader insight into how different characters interpret events.

## Links and further reading

- The trailer for the 2017 film based on *A Monster Calls* is an interesting way to approach the novel with students: https://www.imdb.com/videoplayer/vi1021687321.
- Further information about Patrick Ness and his books can be found on his website at http://patrickness.com/about-me/. There is some personal information about the inspiration for his writing and suggestions for other books to explore.
- Extensive information is available about Bram Stoker, *Dracula* and the vampire myth. A useful link is the British Library at the following page: https://www.bl.uk/romantics-and-victorians/articles/dracula. This site gives access to material that can be used to demonstrate the way the character has been presented through images.
- Students interested in finding out more about Arthurian legends can be guided to *The Orchard Book of Legends of King Arthur* by Andrew Matthews and Peter Utton.
- The original full text of *Sir Gawain and the Green Knight* and alternative translations can be accessed on many websites. The original was written as poetry and some of the translations mirror the alliterative technique and rhyming couplets throughout.
- *Moonfleet* was written at the end of the 19th century with the action set in the late 18th century. Use the following link to learn more about the role of smuggling at the time the novel is set: http://www.smuggling.co.uk/gazetteer_s_15.html.
- Students can find out more about Helen Cresswell's other books at the following link: https://www.goodreads.com/author/list/26835.Helen_Cresswell.

## Planning guidance and teaching tips

Think about how you can make the materials relevant to your students and responsive to their particular needs and learning targets. Some suggested approaches to address key areas are provided below.

- Encourage discussion of students' wider reading wherever possible, particularly in relation to different plots and the creation of a specific atmosphere in a story. Draw on their knowledge of stories that may come from books read earlier in their schooling, even if at primary level. Many lower-attaining students won't have built up much reading stamina or have the confidence or inclination to read independently.
- All the target words are in the target word list at the back of the Student Book. Encourage students to use this to establish the habit of looking up words as part of the process of discussing and exploring their meaning.
- Draw on students' knowledge of action, plot and atmosphere in relation to other forms, such as film and video games, and make links between the common techniques used to create these across different forms of fiction.
- The full narrative of *A Monster Calls* depicts a young boy not coping with the impending death of a parent from cancer, which means care should be taken discussing the issue, depending on what you know about students' personal circumstances and life experiences.
- Refer to the Grammar reference guide on Kerboodle for definitions and exemplars of specific grammar and punctuation terms covered in this chapter. Kerboodle also provides quizzes to help improve the technical accuracy of students' writing and the application of grammar in context.

# Unit focus

## Preparation and resources

- Student Book 1: pages 38–43
- Workbook 1: pages 14–15
- Kerboodle resources:
  - ◊ 2.1 A Monster Calls audio
  - ◊ 2.1 A Monster Calls quiz
  - ◊ 2.1 Word power worksheet
  - ◊ 2.1 Openings worksheet
- Grammatical knowledge: adjective, adverb, noun, phrase, verb
- Key terms: adjective, adverb, atmosphere, context, fiction, imagery, noun (WB), phrase, suspense, verb (WB)

## What this unit teaches and how

- The extract from *A Monster Calls* by Patrick Ness focuses on a boy waking from a recurrent nightmare, only to find another horror waiting for him. The opening is analysed for the use of language to intrigue the reader and create suspense. Text analysis supports later creative writing.

- *Catapult Workbook 1* may also be used to support and develop the skills in this lesson through a short extract from the novel, *The Edge* by Alan Gibbons. The text presents a boy being woken urgently by his mother, and activities draw students' attention to the use of words and phrases to heighten the tension of the scene.

## Skills and objectives

In this unit, students will:

- Explore how a writer creates an effective story opening.

- Practise building suspense and creating a tense atmosphere in their own writing.

- Learn, understand and practise using new vocabulary.

# Teaching suggestions and guidance

This unit is designed to cover two to three lessons, depending on the ability level of your students and the length of lesson time.

### Introduction to the unit (p38)

- Students discuss any experience of recurrent dreams in groups. Gather feedback and make the point that dreams like this can often mean that people have an underlying anxiety.

- Remind students that children often create monsters in their imagination when they feel anxious. You could present an image from *Monsters Inc* as an amusing aside but ensure students understand that the monster is originally a product of fear.

- Collect words that can be used to describe emotions linked to fear, e.g. scared, petrified, frightened, shocked, anxious. These can be kept and used later.

### Engaging with the source text (p39)

- Practise the reading of the text so that the scene is highly dramatic. You could use the first 3 minutes 45 seconds of the clip read by Liam Neeson, who plays the 'monster' in the film: https://www.youtube.com/watch?v=lkrxAYCQi0Q. Alternatively, play the audio recording of the extract on Kerboodle: 2.1 A Monster Calls audio.

- Take feedback from students in response to the 'Ready, set, go!' task in the Student Book. Note that some students may be familiar with the film of the book.

- To test basic comprehension of the extract, ask students to complete the 2.1 A Monster Calls quiz on Kerboodle. This can be completed as a whole-class activity or individually.

**Resources**
- ◊ Kerboodle: 2.1 A Monster Calls audio
- ◊ Kerboodle: 2.1 A Monster Calls quiz

## Word power (pp40-41)

- The activities focus attention on the way the language creates an effective opening to the narrative. For Activity 1a, also ask for some alternative adverbs to 'groggily', e.g. tiredly, exhaustedly.

- Pair work might be productive for completing Activity 3b. If students need prompting, suggest some possible contexts for their sentence, such as being in fog or high winds.

- Target words are also listed in the target word list at the back of the Student Book so encourage students to access this if necessary.

- Encourage students to use the 2.1 Word power worksheet on Kerboodle to help develop and reinforce their vocabulary.

- For Activity 4, discuss déjà vu and suggest sentence starters such as:

  ◇ Something was telling me to be careful but…
  ◇ When I saw her cross the road I recognised her walk – but how?
  ◇ I knew the voice but did not recognise the face…
  ◇ What was that nagging feeling…

**Resources**
◇ Kerboodle: 2.1 Word power worksheet

## Knowledge and understanding (p42)

- Pairs or small groups of students can gather their collective ideas in response to the four activities. Ask one of the pair or group to explain their conclusions.

- Encourage students to explain the answers as if they were writing a sentence and using evidence from the text to justify their response. Discuss the answers and ensure that every student understands why the correct answers are appropriate.

## Writing skills (pp42-43)

- The graph suggested for Activity 2 could be completed on the IWB, with students invited to add their contributions and note them on the board.

- For Activity 3b, remind students of the imbalance of power of someone knowing your name if you do not know them.

- For Activity 4a, remind students of the words they gathered earlier to describe fear. The words may support them in describing the imagery in the given sentence.

- As well as effective words, phrases and punctuation, ask students to consider the effect of the repetition of 'Conor' on separate lines (students may note the lack of speech marks).

- Use the 2.1 Openings worksheet on Kerboodle to explore a variety of powerful story openings and their effect. They are taken from 1 *Mrs Dalloway* by Virginia Woolf; 2 *The Color Purple* by Alice Walker; 3 *Capture the Castle* by Dodie Smith; 4 *1984* by George Orwell; 5 *Metamorphosis* by Franz Kafka; 6 *The Name of the Wind* by Patrick Rothfuss; 7 *The Voyage of the Dawn Treader* by C. S. Lewis; 8 *Jane Eyre* by Charlotte Brontë.

**Resources**
◇ Kerboodle: 2.1 Openings worksheet

## Check your skills (p43)

- Some students may be able to write the next paragraph of the narrative independently, while others may benefit from further discussion and support for ideas and vocabulary prior to their writing. If necessary, recap on possible uses of the target words and guide towards the development of phrases such as 'he stumbled groggily', 'straining to see out of the window', '… had a monstrous quality'.

- The following sentence starters could be used to support students' writing:

  ◇ Conor's dream had left the boundaries of his mind and…
  ◇ 'Am I still asleep?' he thought as the sound of the creaking wood grew louder…
  ◇ He did not know what to expect, what to say or what to do…
  ◇ The panic returned and held his chest in a vice-like grip…

## Unit focus

### Preparation and resources

- Student Book 1: pages 44–49
- Workbook 1: pages 16–17
- Kerboodle resources:
  ◇ 2.2 Dracula audio
  ◇ 2.2 Dracula quiz
  ◇ 2.2 Word power worksheet
  ◇ 2.2 Character worksheet
- Grammatical knowledge: clause, multi-clause sentence
- Key terms: atmosphere (WB), clause, dialogue, multi-clause sentence, narrator, novel, sentence structure, setting (WB), structure

### What this unit teaches and how

- The extract from the text *Dracula* by Bram Stoker offers the opportunity to focus on the meaning of some archaic language. Further activities help students to analyse how sentence structure can help to create mood and atmosphere, leading to guidance for their own creative writing.

- *Catapult Workbook 1* may also be used to support and develop the skills in this unit through analysing an extract from *The Woman in Black* by Susan Hill, which is written in the style of a traditional Gothic novel.

### Skills and objectives

In this unit, students will:

- Explore how sentence structures contribute to mood and atmosphere.

- Learn, understand and practise using new vocabulary.

# Teaching suggestions and guidance

This unit is designed to cover two to three lessons, depending on the ability level of your students and the length of lesson time.

### Introduction to the unit (p44)

- Project a series of images depicting Count Dracula from different published versions of the text and film.

- Ask students to create spider diagrams including all their knowledge about Count Dracula and/or vampires. Give them five minutes.

### Engaging with the source text (p45)

- This extract will be challenging for some lower-attaining students so do not ask them to read it by themselves. Instead, read the extract aloud to students in a dramatic/melodramatic style so that the Gothic nature of the text is highlighted. The exclamation marks give great opportunities for this. Include a strong accent for Count Dracula. You could also act out the actions described, such as miming the throwing of the mirror through the window. Alternatively, play the audio recording of the extract on Kerboodle: 2.2 Dracula audio.

- Take feedback from the 'Ready, set, go!' task, focusing on how the details in this extract comply with traditional expectations of vampires.

- To test basic comprehension of the extract, ask students to complete the 2.2 Dracula quiz on Kerboodle. This can be completed as a whole-class activity or individually.

**Resources**
◇ Kerboodle: 2.2 Dracula audio
◇ Kerboodle: 2.2 Dracula quiz

## Word power (pp46–47)

- For Activity 1a, the focus is on the third paragraph and the lack of a reflection. The appropriate answer for Activity 1b is 'alarmed'. Ask students for synonyms, e.g. shocked, amazed.

- For Activity 4, ask students whether 'wrench' is being used as a verb or noun (a noun, even though it describes a movement). Ask for appropriate adjectives to describe this movement, e.g. violent, ruthless, dramatic, forceful.

- For Activity 5, encourage students to experiment with ideas for Harker's speech with a partner, before writing it down.

- Use the 2.2 Word power worksheet on Kerboodle to help students explore the target words and some of the archaic vocabulary in this extract.

**Resource**
◊ Kerboodle: 2.2 Word power worksheet

## Knowledge and understanding (p48)

- Ask students to work in pairs on each question so that they can compare answers. It may be helpful to gain plenary feedback after each question.

- Ensure students can back up their answers with close reference to the text.

## Writing skills (pp48–49)

- Use the 2.2 Character worksheet on Kerboodle to explore the presentation of Dracula's character.

- For Activity 1, offer the following suggestions to start students thinking: sinister, frightening, worrying, threatening.

- In Activity 2, do not allow students to become over-anxious about grammatical terms but ensure they recognise that long, multi-clause sentences can help to build up mood and atmosphere in a description. Some revision of grammatical terms may be helpful in the analysis of the example given.

**Resource**
◊ Kerboodle: 2.2 Character worksheet

## Check your skills (p49)

- If students require more support, a group activity can generate some vocabulary and ideas for this task, e.g. echoing steps, draughts in the corridor, change in temperature, strange shadows, flickering candlelight, gloomy rooms, dilapidated windows and doors, whispers and distant cries. Remind students to use a variety of sentence types (long and short) to vary the tension in the narrative.

- Some students might find the following sentence starters helpful, in addition to the one given in the Student Book:

  ◊ With much fear in my heart, I decided to discover more about…
  ◊ Every part of my soul screamed at me to leave, but…
  ◊ Even the walls of the castle seemed to watch my every move as…
  ◊ Certain that the Count had more secrets in store, I…

# Unit focus

## Preparation and resources

- Student Book 1: pages 50–55
- Workbook 1: pages 18–19
- Kerboodle resources:
  ◊ 2.3 Sir Gawain and the Green Knight audio
  ◊ 2.3 Sir Gawain and the Green Knight quiz
  ◊ 2.3 Word power worksheet
  ◊ 2.3 Alliteration worksheet
- Grammatical knowledge: Noun, verb
- Key terms: alliteration, metaphor, phrase (WB), poetic language

## What this unit teaches and how

- The extract from *Sir Gawain and the Green Knight,* retold by Michael Morpurgo, is a dramatic presentation of power and fear. Activities focus on the writing techniques used in the depiction of character and give students the opportunity to use these techniques in their own writing.

- *Catapult Workbook 1* supports and develops the skills in this unit through an extract from *Beowulf,* also retold by Michael Morpurgo. Activities focus on what we can infer from the reaction of characters to each other and the effect of alliteration in the text.

## Skills and objectives

In this unit, students will:

- Explore how a writer describes a dramatic event through description.

- Use alliteration and other techniques to create an effective description of a character.

- Learn, understand and practise using new vocabulary.

# Teaching suggestions and guidance

This unit is designed to cover two to three lessons, depending on the ability level of your students and the length of lesson time.

### Introduction to the unit (p50)

- Explore what students know about the Arthurian legends and knighthood. Groups can create six key points and then give feedback to the rest of the class. The answers may include references to ideas such as 'armour' and 'Excalibur'. Ensure an understanding that knighthood exemplified what it was to be a 'good' person (morally pure) who defended the innocent and fought evil.

- Tell students to keep the words and ideas, and add to them through the unit, as they will make use of some or all of them in later activities.

### Engaging with the source text (p51)

- Discuss why this text is 'retold' (to make it accessible to a modern reader). You could display the following from the original text:
  *And all graythed in grene this gome and his wedes:*
  *A strayt cote ful streght that stek on his sides,*

  (These lines are mirrored at the start of the extract's second paragraph). Point out that it is one of the earliest known examples of written *poetic* English.

- Play the audio recording of the extract on Kerboodle: 2.3 Sir Gawain and the Green Knight audio.

- Take feedback on the 'Ready, set go!' task, asking students why they think this is such a dramatic entry for a character. They might comment on his physical power and size, surprising appearance, and the reaction of the other people and dogs.

- To test basic comprehension of the extract, ask students to complete the 2.3 Sir Gawain and the Green Knight quiz on Kerboodle. This can be completed as a whole-class activity or individually.

**Resources**
◊ Kerboodle: 2.3 Sir Gawain and the Green Knight audio
◊ Kerboodle: 2.3 Sir Gawain and the Green Knight quiz

## Word power (pp52-53)

- Target words are also listed in the target word list at the back of the Student Book, so encourage students to access this if necessary.

- Revise word classes to extend students in Activity 1. Focus on the use of the word 'gape' as a verb and 'scowl' as a noun. Remind students that many words can belong to more than one word class ('gape' and 'scowl' can be used as both a noun and a verb in different contexts). Ask students to think of alternative words, e.g. stare, grimace. The 2.3 Word power worksheet on Kerboodle contains activities to support this word class work.

- Activity 4 is based on the contrast between the knight's awesome appearance and the fact that he carries a sprig of holly, which is again contrasted with his heavy weaponry.

- In Activity 5, students write a description of a mythical creature. Model some ideas using the image of the dragon, including some target words, such as: massive wingspan, gaping jaws, staring eyes, terrifying shriek.

- Share reading the examples around the class and encourage students to make them as dramatic as possible!

**Resources**
◊ Kerboodle: 2.3 Word power worksheet

## Knowledge and understanding (p54)

- To support students in Activity 2, direct them to the third paragraph of the text and encourage them to think about the horse's size, colour and mood/temperament.

- Ensure that students understand 'widow maker' from Activity 3. Draw attention to the fact that all knights and warriors were men.

- When discussing Activities 4 and 5, ask students whether they think the Green Knight's power is from his confidence and physical presence or from some form of supernatural power.

## Writing skills (p55)

- Use the 2.3 Alliteration worksheet on Kerboodle to reinforce students' understanding of alliteration.

- Project again the lines taken from the original text shown earlier in the lesson. Highlight the text to show students how the medieval alliterative technique worked:
  *And all graythed in grene this gome and his wedes:*
  *A strayt cote ful streght that stek on his sides,*

- Support students in Activity 1b by offering an example, such as: The wild wind swirled around the Knight, whisking up leaves that spun around him.

- Ask students how often they use the word 'awesome' and what they mean by it. Compare their responses with the traditional meaning of 'awesome' as defined in the Tip panel.

**Resources**
◊ Kerboodle: 2.3 Alliteration worksheet

## Check your skills (p55)

- Remind students of the words and ideas linked to knighthood that they collected in the first part of the lesson. They may wish to use these in their writing.

- Remind students that their description of how the other characters respond to the Green Knight can reflect the power and impact that he has on the gathering.

- Students may find the following sentence starters helpful:

  ◊ Nobody chose to challenge the champion dressed in green…
  ◊ Fear gripped the room…
  ◊ King Arthur knew that his honour was at stake…

# Unit focus

## Preparation and resources

- Student Book 1: pages 56–61
- Workbook 1: pages 20–21
- Kerboodle resources:
  ◇ 2.4 Moonfleet audio
  ◇ 2.4 Moonfleet quiz
  ◇ 2.4 Word power worksheet
  ◇ 2.4 Extended metaphor worksheet
- Key term: extended metaphor, suspense (WB), synonym

## What this unit teaches and how

- The extract from *Moonfleet* by J. Meade Falkner describes a boy caught in a dangerous situation. The activities focus on some of the techniques that the author uses to build suspense. Students are then given the opportunity to write an analysis of these techniques and their effects.

- *Catapult Workbook 1* supports and develops the skills in this lesson through an extract from *Wild Boy* by Rob Lloyd Jones. Students analyse how the description of fog descending on a city can build suspense and tension.

## Skills and objectives

In this unit, students will:

- Identify how the sequencing of events can build suspense.

- Explore how an extended metaphor and other techniques can be used to build suspense.

- Learn, understand and practise using new vocabulary.

# Teaching suggestions and guidance

This unit is designed to cover two to three lessons, depending on the ability level of your students and the length of lesson time.

### Introduction to the unit (p56)

- Ask students to describe to a partner or small group a time that they felt trapped. This could have been in a physical place, a confrontation or a dilemma, e.g. not wishing to visit a relative or having to explain why homework hasn't been done.

- Ask students to note down the five most appropriate words to describe their feelings. Gather feedback and tell students to retain their words for future activities.

### Engaging with the source text (p57)

- Ensure students understand what smuggling was (the illegal importing of goods, which evaded official channels and therefore tax). It was rife in coastal areas in the 18th century, where goods such as wine, brandy, tea, coffee, salt, leather and soap were frequently smuggled inland, involving whole communities in the illegal trade. Project a picture on the IWB of smugglers on a beach.

- Read the text aloud or, alternatively, play the audio recording of the extract on Kerboodle: 2.4 Moonfleet audio.

- Take feedback on the 'Ready, set, go!' task. You might want to give students a copy of the text (or display it on the IWB) for them to highlight the part that would make them most fearful if they were in John's shoes.

- To test basic comprehension of the extract, ask students to complete the 2.4 Moonfleet quiz on Kerboodle. This can be completed as a whole-class activity or individually.

**Resources**
◇ Kerboodle: 2.4 Moonfleet audio
◇ Kerboodle: 2.4 Moonfleet quiz

## Word power (pp58-59)

- To reinforce understanding in Activity 1a, ask students to write a sentence using 'defined' in the sense of clarity of sight rather than sound. You could offer the starter: 'As I got nearer to the ship…'.

- Encourage students to respond to Activity 2 by explaining the quotation integrated into a sentence, e.g. John's extreme fear is (portrayed/ depicted/described)….

- Activities 3a and 3b are closely linked. If necessary, remind students that life was violent and dangerous, and smugglers faced severe penalties if they were discovered. Answers should be in less than 30 words, including integrated quotations.

- Before students respond to Activity 4, encourage discussion as to whether they would resist the temptation to pry if put in the situation outlined. Use the following sentence starters to support students if necessary:

  ◇ I asked myself whether I should read, and…
  ◇ I struggled with my conscience, but…
  ◇ My head told me to resist, but my heart shouted, 'Read it!', then…

- Use the 2.4 Word power worksheet on Kerboodle to reinforce and develop students' confidence with the archaic language used in the source text for this unit.

**Resources**
◇ Kerboodle: 2.4 Word power worksheet

## Knowledge and understanding (p60)

- This section demands information retrieval skills and could be completed in pairs.

- In order to respond to Activity 4 fully, you may need to explain about the role of the Church in the 18th century and its high status in the society of the day. Also draw out that not many people would have wanted to visit church vaults.

- Draw attention to the image and question in the caption. Ensure students understand fully that smuggling was lucrative and widespread.

Emphasise that poverty in the 18th century was rife and life was very harsh in coastal towns and villages, so the opportunity to engage in smuggling was very tempting. It provided people with much-needed money.

## Reading skills (pp60-61)

- Support Activity 2 by asking students whether they think John is being presented in a negative or positive way. Then ask them to create a spider diagram that includes evidence to support their views. Finally, encourage them to relate their views in full sentences either orally or in writing.

- In responding to Activity 3c, some students may benefit from possible sentence starters:

  ◇ Fear is described through…
  ◇ John compares his situation to…
  ◇ The sense of being trapped is emphasised by…

- Use the 2.4 Extended metaphor worksheet on Kerboodle to explore and reinforce students' understanding of this concept.

**Resources**
◇ Kerboodle: 2.4 Extended metaphor worksheet

## Check your skills (p61)

- Remind students to use short integrated quotations in support of their ideas. The following sentence structures could be modelled to support students' use of integrated evidence:

  ◇ Tension is created by…
  ◇ The words… and… show that…
  ◇ The reader is left in suspense because…
  ◇ When John, as narrator, explains that he feels…, this shows that…
  ◇ We can share the tension with the narrator as…

- Encourage students to peer-assess each other's work, in pairs, using the final three bullets as a mini-checklist of features.

# Unit focus

## Preparation and resources

- Student Book 1: pages 62–67
- Workbook 1: pages 22–23
- Kerboodle resources:
  ◇ 2.5 Moondial audio
  ◇ 2.5 Moondial quiz
  ◇ 2.5 Word power worksheet
  ◇ 2.5 Narrative viewpoint worksheet
- Key terms: imperative (WB), imply, personification, second-person narrative, simile

## What this unit teaches and how

- The extract from the text *Moondial* by Helen Cresswell is used to focus on how to create a mysterious atmosphere. A place is portrayed from the perspective of a young girl, convinced that there is more to it than meets the eye.

- *Catapult Workbook 1* supports and develops the skills in this lesson through an extract from *A Thief in the House of Memory* by Tim Wynne-Jones. The text offers further ideas for how to structure a narrative that directly addresses the reader.

## Skills and objectives

In this unit, students will:

- Identify key details and show awareness of implied meaning.

- Explore how narrative perspective, similes and personification can be used to create a mysterious atmosphere in their own writing.

- Learn, understand and practise using new vocabulary.

# Teaching suggestions and guidance

This unit is designed to cover two to three lessons, depending on the ability level of your students and the length of lesson time.

### Introduction to the unit (p62)

- Ask students to discuss, in small groups or pairs, a personal experience when they were frightened by something that they can't explain. Share some experiences with the whole class.

- Use an experience of your own (real or imagined) to demonstrate how tension can be developed by addressing your audience as you recount the event. For example:

  ◇ Have you ever been out late on a cold winter's night?
  ◇ Do you know that feeling that you're being watched?
  ◇ Has your heartbeat sounded loud in your ears as you walk along?
  ◇ Do you know that feeling of being followed?

- Point out how this direct address engages the audience in a very immediate way. Explain that some writers use this direct address in novels. If appropriate, introduce the term 'second-person narrative', emphasising that 'you' is the second-person pronoun.

### Engaging with the source text (p63)

- The extract from *Moondial* involves the reader in a similar way to an oral storyteller addressing their audience, by using the second person (you) throughout. Read the text using as much dramatic tension as possible; pause after the interrogative, e.g. 'what then?' Alternatively, play the audio recording of the extract on Kerboodle: 2.5 Moondial audio.

- Take brief feedback from the 'Ready, set, go!' task, which asks students to consider how the author appeals to all the senses. If necessary, recap the five senses of seeing, smelling, touching, hearing and tasting.

- To test basic comprehension of the extract, ask students to complete the 2.5 Moondial quiz on Kerboodle. This can be completed as a whole-class activity or individually.

**Resources**
◇ Kerboodle: 2.5 Moondial audio
◇ Kerboodle: 2.5 Moondial quiz

## Word power (pp64–65)

- In Activity 1, ensure that students understand the difference between 'loom' and 'jump out'.

- In Activity 2, support students in understanding the subtlety of 'half dreading' describing a state of only just staying in control.

- Introduce the term 'ESP' (extra sensory perception) in Activity 3. Link it to the idea of the 'sixth sense' in the question and the discussion about unexplained experiences. For Activity 3a, emphasise the difference between 'imply' (based on what is said) and 'infer' (based on interpretation). Focus on the role of the supernatural in Activities 3b and 3c.

- Complete Activity 4 collaboratively. Use the caption to prompt students to speculate as to what might happen next. Ask students to write their first two lines and then compare them with a partner. Decide on the best bits and then write the rest together before feedback. The following sentence starters could be given for support:

  ◇ I looked up and wondered what lay above in that room…
  ◇ Countless feet had stood here before me…
  ◇ What would I find when…
  ◇ I knew that I could not change the past but…

- Use 2.5 Word power worksheet on Kerboodle to explore homonyms and synonyms of the target vocabulary.

**Resources**
◇ Kerboodle: 2.5 Word power worksheet

## Knowledge and understanding (p66)

- Support students in Activity 1 by offering sentence starters, such as:

  ◇ The night is given human characteristics by the narrator, who explains that…
  ◇ The narrator is not literally 'blindfolded', but the night…

- For Activity 4, students could be given copies of the text and work in pairs to highlight any evidence of any senses being described.

- If students need prompting for Activity 5, you could start by offering some vocabulary such as: decaying, ancient, frozen, solid.

## Writing skills (p67)

- Use the 2.5 Narrative viewpoint worksheet on Kerboodle to reinforce students' understanding of different narrative perspectives. Explore how the second person directly involves the reader, almost as a fellow participant in the experience.

- Activities 2 and 3 involve discussion of imagery. Link these with the earlier discussion about 'blindfolded'. If appropriate, remind students of the key features of similes and personification.

**Resources**
◇ Kerboodle: 2.5 Narrative viewpoint worksheet

## Check your skills (p67)

- Give students two different pre-prepared examples of response, one much weaker than the other, perhaps missing criteria. The examples could be analysed before students attempt their own writing. A word limit of 100 words will help to focus thinking.

- In addition (or alternatively), offer students the following suggested sentence starters:

  ◇ All my senses were fighting for attention as…
  ◇ I struggled to hold my nerve when…
  ◇ Part of me was dreading what I might find but…
  ◇ I felt a presence loom over me…

# Assessment suggestions and guidance

## Why are we assessing this?

Students have completed the chapter on Action and atmosphere, exploring these aspects through a variety of high-quality contemporary, 20th- and pre-20th-century fiction texts. The units have reinforced and developed the essential reading and writing skills outlined below, consolidating knowledge and increasing students' confidence.

This assessment unit gives students and teachers the opportunity to assess and reflect on how firmly these skills – in particular, the writing skills – have been grasped and how effectively students can employ them in an assessment situation.

## What are students demonstrating?

Students are asked to:

- build suspense and create a tense atmosphere
- use alliteration and other techniques to describe a character
- describe a sequence of events that suggests excitement and suspense
- use similes, metaphors and personification to create a mysterious atmosphere
- use some of the target words covered in this chapter.

## How to deliver the assessment

- Writing extended texts under pressure of time can be challenging for lower-attaining students. The level of support required will vary, depending on students' needs and confidence.
- Ensure that all students are clear about what is required for the task before they start work on it. Discuss the suggested stages of planning, drafting and editing, and recap on the writing techniques they are expected to use.
- Ideally, the assessment should be completed in one session but, for students who require most support, it may be helpful to split it into stages, with some verbal prompts between stages and the writing of paragraphs. This staged approach will build the confidence of weaker students as they see their skills develop.

- Students could each choose one of the three tasks or all could work on the same task to enable whole-class planning and preparation.
- If students would benefit from sentence starters, you could provide the following options:

### Task A

- ◇ I controlled my nerves in the way that I had been trained…
- ◇ Did I feel anxious? Yes, but I had to…
- ◇ What was actually just a brief moment seemed to last…
- ◇ The cold ice of fear began to melt as I realised…

### Task B

- ◇ The threadbare clothes barely hung together on its…
- ◇ At that precise moment, the voice of my mother murmured in my mind…
- ◇ The words that fell from its mouth have haunted me to this day because…
- ◇ The surprised students sat in silence as…

### Task C

- ◇ The battle-scarred walls spoke to me of…
- ◇ You walk down a dark corridor, blasted by the cold wind, you find…
- ◇ I heard the scratching of mice, touched the rough stone and felt…
- ◇ There was nothing there, but I knew, I just knew that…

## How to mark the assessment

You will want to mark this in line with departmental and school marking guidelines. If you wish, you could use the *Catapult* marking scales (provided on Kerboodle). The *Catapult* marking scales are designed to assess lower-attaining students who need to consolidate skills that have not yet been fully grasped but need to be secured and developed in order to move those students forward and narrow the gap between their existing levels of achievement and national expectations for KS3.

Using the *Catapult* marking scales will help you to identify specific strengths and areas for improvement in an individual student's writing. This may help you to set development targets as well as building a profile of your class as writers.

## Following up the assessment

The assessment should enable you to identify clear areas in which students have underperformed and you can therefore plan in detail how to reinforce understanding using *Catapult* resources.

1. Refer to the *Catapult* mapping grids on pages 132-135 of this Teacher Book to identify other *Catapult* chapters where these reading and writing skills are covered. For example:

   ◊ techniques to describe a character are also covered in Chapter 1 (Unit 5)
   ◊ metaphors are also covered in Chapter 5 (Unit 1).

2. Direct students to the SPaG quizzes on Kerboodle to address any areas of weakness that the assessment may have revealed. For example, basic skills can be reinforced with the following quizzes:

   ◊ Capital letters
   ◊ Full stops
   ◊ Commas
   ◊ Sentences.

   Encourage students to proofread their work, looking for ways of making their writing style more concise and fluent. For example, skills can be reinforced with the following quizzes:

   ◊ Noun phrases
   ◊ Adverbials
   ◊ Adjectives
   ◊ Adverbs
   ◊ Conjunctions
   ◊ Parenthesis
   ◊ Verbs and tenses.

   The Grammar reference guide on Kerboodle contains definitions and additional examples of each of the spelling, punctuation and grammar points covered in the quizzes, for your reference.

3. If students' vocabulary seems limited, remind them to make use of the target words they have explored, which are also contained in the target word list at the back of the Student Book. Students may also benefit from compiling their own vocabulary lists for reference. These should be shared and discussed regularly.

4. If spelling is problematic, encourage regular revision of common spelling patterns in frequently used words, e.g. the 'igh' spelling for words containing the long 'i' sound, e.g. fright, night, delight; the 'ph' spelling for the sound 'f', e.g. phone, phrase, apostrophe; contractions in which missing letters are replaced by an apostrophe, e.g. can't, I'll, we've.

5. Ensure students are competent at spelling high-frequency words, particularly those that are commonly misspelt, e.g. recognise, because, system, its/it's, across, achieve, believe, individual, completely, muscle, finally, friend, immediately, separate, remember, truly, surprise, weird, fortunately, therefore, successful, tomorrow. Encourage strategies to learn these spellings, using mnemonics, chanting, singing, repetition and any other ways that help to embed the knowledge.

### Resources
◊ Kerboodle: *Catapult* marking scales
◊ Kerboodle: SPaG quizzes
◊ Kerboodle: Grammar reference guide

Note that the source texts and activities in *Catapult Workbook 1* can also be used as assessment material, if students haven't already used them to consolidate their learning from the Student Book.

# Chapter 3: Explanations and insights

## Chapter overview

### Why are we teaching this?

Understanding how writers present information in a clear, concise way is fundamental in appreciating non-fiction. By exploring high-quality texts, selected to be accessible and appealing, students can then develop their own writing through carefully supported activities.

Across the four units and in the final assessment in this chapter, students will read a range of non-fiction texts from *All about the Telephone and Phonograph*, written in 1878, to a newspaper article from 2016 introducing readers to the concept of delivery robots. Students are given an opportunity to use the analytical skills they have practised in the reading assessment at the end of the chapter.

Many activities in this chapter will benefit from discussion prior to students completing a written response. Encourage students to elaborate and explain clearly their understanding and ideas. Speaking and listening skills are an important prerequisite to developing effective reading and writing skills, so they should be an integral part of each unit.

### What are the learning aims?

In every unit in this chapter, students will learn to strengthen the core skills of:

- learning, understanding and practising using new vocabulary
- increasing general knowledge and contextual understanding.

In addition, units will focus on the following learning aims. Students will:

| Unit 1 | Unit 2 | Unit 3 | Unit 4 |
|---|---|---|---|
| • Identify key information in a text.<br>• Use subheadings and paragraphs to organise information and ideas.<br>• Learn, understand and practise using new vocabulary. | • Find relevant information from different parts of a text.<br>• Combine information to develop and demonstrate overall understanding.<br>• Learn, understand and practise using new vocabulary. | • Understand how a writer uses sentence structure and paragraphs to make information interesting and relevant to the reader.<br>• Practise writing their own informative and relevant news report.<br>• Learn, understand and practise using new vocabulary. | • Gather information from a 19th-century text.<br>• Understand how sentence forms, punctuation and language choices are used to communicate meaning and tone in a 19th-century text.<br>• Learn, understand and practise using new vocabulary. |

### How will this chapter be assessed?

The reading assessment at the end of the chapter uses texts about Ada Lovelace to help students practise the reading analysis skills developed throughout the chapter.

The focus for assessment will be:

- identifying key information
- analysing how language is used to convey meaning and tone
- combining information to develop and demonstrate overall understanding.

Note that the short 'Check your skills' feature at the end of every unit in this chapter provides formative assessment opportunities to support students' learning.

## Chapter 3 unit sequence

The sequence of units is designed so that students gain in confidence as they complete more challenging activities while progressing through the chapter. Some units build upon skills introduced in previous units, reinforcing and extending students' learning.

Note that some activities feature in just the Teacher Book (TB).

<table>
<tr><th colspan="3">Chapter 3:<br>Explanations and insights</th></tr>
<tr><td></td><td>Student Book</td><td>Workbook</td></tr>
<tr>
<td>1: Understanding robots</td>
<td>Source text: 'Robotics: Facts'<br><br>• Discuss the changing image and role of robots in our lives. (TB)<br>• Explore the ways that words work in context.<br>• Write an explanation of the suitability of robots for specific jobs.<br>• Write an entry for website explaining modern technology, using appropriate subheadings and paragraphing.</td>
<td>Source text: 'Nanorobots'<br><br>• Group information into paragraphs.<br>• Write a text using topic sentences.</td>
</tr>
<tr>
<td>2: Learning about the past</td>
<td>Source text: 'Mary Anning, discoverer of prehistoric fossils'<br><br>• Discuss the meanings of biography and autobiography. (TB)<br>• Find specific information drawn from the whole text to answer questions.<br>• Use information from the text to explore Mary Anning's personality.<br>• Write about aspects of 19th-century life based on what has been learned from the text.</td>
<td>Source text: Extract from A Short Biographical Dictionary of English Literature<br><br>• Use scanning skills to locate relevant information.<br>• Write concise information in chronological order.</td>
</tr>
<tr>
<td>3: Reporting the future</td>
<td>Source text: Extract from 'Delivery robots to replace takeaway drivers in London trial'<br><br>• Explain how technology is a vital part of everyday life from an individual student perspective. (TB)<br>• Write an imaginative account of 'meeting' a delivery robot in the local high street, using target words.<br>• Write an article using structural features exemplified in the text, including a strong opening, quotations from developers and short information-packed paragraphs.</td>
<td>Source text: Extract from 'Meet the one-eyed robot – it's fantastic'<br><br>• Identify information that dates an article.<br>• Write the opening of an article designed to catch attention.</td>
</tr>
<tr>
<td>4: A modern marvel</td>
<td>Source text: Extract from All About the Telephone and Phonograph<br><br>• Discuss 19th-century technological advances and how they changed people's lives. (TB)<br>• Explore how the language style expresses the writer's attitude and tone.<br>• Write a letter in the role of a 19th-century enthusiast of new technology.<br>• Explore the lexical density of 19th-century text, in particular multi-clause sentences.<br>• Write an analysis of the way the writer explains their feelings about the new technology.</td>
<td>Source text: Extract from 'The Making of a Tunnel – the Waterloo and City Railway'<br><br>• Compare archaic language with modern expressions.<br>• Explore the effects of using the active and passive voice.</td>
</tr>
</table>

| Chapter 3:<br>Explanations and insights | |
|---|---|
| Student Book | Workbook |

<table>
<tr><td rowspan="2" style="writing-mode:vertical">Reading assesment</td><td>Source text 1: 'The world's first computer programmer (1815–1852)'<br><br>Source text 2: 'Ada Lovelace fact file'</td><td></td></tr>
<tr><td><ul><li>Identify key information.</li><li>Analyse how language is used to convey meaning and tone.</li><li>Combine information to develop and demonstrate overall understanding.</li></ul></td><td></td></tr>
</table>

# Preparing to teach

## Refresh your knowledge

You might find it helpful to refer to the following key points when planning the teaching of this chapter:

- The imagery of robots has been used over the last century or so to signify the rise of technology. One of the most famous historical robot images is of the mechanised replacement for Maria in Fritz Lang's *Metropolis* (1927). In literature, the robot has historically been portrayed as a threat to mankind and given a hostile character due to the lack of emotion. More recently portrayed robot characters include the more empathy-inducing replicants in *Blade Runner*, the robot companions in *Star Wars*, and heroic characters in their own right, e.g. WALL.E

- Students could be introduced to Isaac Asimov's 'Three Laws of Robotics', which originally appeared in *I, Robot* by Asimov, written in 1950:

  1. A robot may not injure a human being or, through inaction, allow a human being to come to harm.
  2. A robot must obey orders given to it by human beings except where such orders would conflict with the First Law.
  3. A robot must protect its own existence as long as such protection does not conflict with the First or Second Law.

- Nineteenth-century technology developed communication and travel, making the world seem smaller. Scientists could collaborate and compete with each other, quickly becoming aware of others' successes. This spurred on scientific enquiry. It may be helpful to look at the way the 20th-century world became obsessed with material goods for the home and labour-saving gadgets.

## Links and further reading

- Background information about the use of robotics in industries such as car manufacture can be found on industry-specific websites, e.g. https://www.mbtmag.com/article/2016/03/how-technology-changing-automotive-industry-2016.
- A fascinating look at the kind of jobs that will disappear in 20 years' time can be researched in an article from *The Guardian* in 2017: https://www.theguardian.com/us-news/2017/jun/26/jobs-future-automation-robots-skills-creative-health.

- Students wishing to find out more about Mary Anning in an accessible text can search out *Mary Anning* (History VIPs) by Kay Barnham (2016). Depending on students' ability, the BBC primary website gives some simple information at: http://www.bbc.co.uk/ schools/primaryhistory/famouspeople/mary_anning/. A more detailed biographical page dealing with the life of Mary Anning can be found at: http://www.ucmp.berkeley. edu/history/anning.html.
- Students may enjoy looking at some of the people who are rated as inventing the most important 19th-century technological breakthroughs at: http://historylists. org/people/10-greatest-inventors-of-the-19th-century.html. This includes Alexander Graham Bell (telephone) and Samuel Morse (telegraph and Morse Code). However, possibly even more important in terms of being far ahead of her time was Ada Lovelace, now acknowledged as the first theoretical computer programmer – over 100 years before anyone else! Students can find out more at: https://www.biography. com/people/ada-lovelace-20825323.

## Planning guidance and teaching tips

Think about how you can make the materials relevant to your students and responsive to their particular needs and learning targets. Some suggested approaches to address key areas are provided below.

- Encourage students to read a range of newspapers and news material (online and in print) so that they can start to draw their own conclusions about whether articles designed to report information (or facts) ever become persuasive or manipulative. They should also be given tasks that entail research of famous individuals and/or someone/something from the past. Select the subjects carefully – even ask specific questions to which students need to find the answers to present to the group.
- All the target words are in the target word list at the back of the Student Book. Encourage students to use this to establish the habit of looking up words as part of the process of discussing and exploring their meaning.
- Focus on developing critical perspective in students to help them become more selective in their own reading and to decide how much they trust what they read. For instance, when looking at the text *All about the Telephone and Phonograph* in Unit 4, students could be asked whether it could be seen as a type of advertisement for the technology.
- Students could be asked what kind of non-fiction texts pass on information most efficiently and effectively. How much do students want to read if they are looking for an answer to a question? Assess the ability of students to skim read for key points in a document by only giving a limited time to scan. This can be adapted by giving students the same document for 30 seconds but with different areas highlighted/ emboldened. This will demonstrate how a text (certainly websites) can fool the brain by drawing the eye towards particular sections of text (web links to other stories).
- Refer to the Grammar reference guide on Kerboodle for definitions and examples of specific grammatical features covered by this chapter. Kerboodle also provides quizzes to help improve the technical accuracy of students' writing and the application of grammar in context.

# Unit focus

## Preparation and resources

- Student Book 1: pages 70–75
- Workbook 1: pages 24–25
- Kerboodle resources:
  ◇ 3.1 Robotics: Facts audio
  ◇ 3.1 Robotics: Facts quiz
  ◇ 3.1 Word power worksheet
  ◇ 3.1 Meaning in sentences worksheet
- Grammatical knowledge: adjective
- Key terms: adjective, conjunction (WB), non-fiction, subheading, summary, topic sentence (WB)

## What this unit teaches and how

- The webpage text, 'Robotics: Facts' offers a rationale for the acceptance of robots replacing humans in many roles. The activities look at the language, vocabulary and presentation of information in the extract and provide students with an opportunity to write their own short encyclopaedia entry, using similar features.

- *Catapult Workbook 1* supports and develops the skills in this unit through another extract from the webpage 'Robotics: Facts'. The text describes the technology behind the potential role of nanorobots in our future lives.

## Skills and objectives

In this unit, students will:

- Identify key information in a text.
- Use subheadings and paragraphs to organise information and ideas.
- Learn, understand and practise using new vocabulary.

# Teaching suggestions and guidance

This unit is designed to cover two to three lessons, depending on the ability level of your students and the length of lesson time.

### Introduction to the unit (p70)

- Ask students what kind of texts they use to find out facts and information. Discuss looking at sources and how reliable they might be.

- Project a picture of a 1950s sci-fi film robot. Ask students to discuss what they think about this image of a robot. Discuss the current roles of robots in our lives. Ask groups to create spider diagrams on the roles discussed and keep these for use later in the unit.

### Engaging with the source text (p71)

- Ask students to read the text in groups and to highlight or note any unfamiliar words. Discuss these words in a plenary. Alternatively, play the audio recording of the extract on Kerboodle: 3.1 Robotics: Facts audio.

- Take feedback on ideas in response to the 'Ready, set, go!' task in the Student Book. Draw out how subheadings divide up the text, making it look less dense, and how they flag the type of information grouped in the paragraph below, making it easier to locate specific information.

- To test basic comprehension of the extract, ask students to complete the 3.1 Robotics: Facts quiz on Kerboodle. This can be completed as a whole-class activity or individually.

**Resources**
◇ Kerboodle: 3.1 Robotics: Facts audio
◇ Kerboodle: 3.1 Robotics: Facts quiz

## Word power (pp72-73)

- For Activity 1a, ask students to think of an alternative word for 'ideal' (e.g. appropriate, perfect) and create sentences that demonstrate its use.

- If appropriate, extend Activity 2 by asking students which adjective and adverb are formed from the word 'tactics' (tactical, tactically). Ask them to use these words in sentences to show their understanding.

- Encourage students to use the 3.1 Word power worksheet on Kerboodle to help develop their understanding of further vocabulary from the source text. This worksheet introduces homographs (words that are spelt the same but have more than one meaning).

**Resources**
◊ Kerboodle: 3.1 Word power worksheet

## Knowledge and understanding (p73)

- Students could work in pairs to complete the activities in this section, then share with the whole class.

- For Activity 3, give a limit of 25 words. Ask students to write their answer on a sticky note so that these can be read together.

- For Activity 4, further practise the effect of using inverted commas in this way by asking students to create a sentence using the word 'friend' in inverted commas.

## Writing skills (pp74-75)

- Use the 3.1 Meaning in sentences worksheet on Kerboodle to reinforce students' understanding of topic sentences and how they are used most effectively.

- For Activity 3, give a maximum of 100 words for the writing task. If necessary, offer some sentence starters:

  ◊ Robots are important in many jobs because…
  ◊ We rely more and more on robot technology because…

**Resources**
◊ Kerboodle: 3.1 Meaning in sentences worksheet

## Check your skills (p75)

- Ensure students understand the nature of the task and that an encyclopaedia is a collection of factual information about many different subjects, usually arranged in alphabetical order. (Wikipedia is a type of online encyclopaedia.)

- If students struggle with ideas for subheadings, guide them towards some possibilities, such as 'History', 'What they can do', 'Types of phones'.

- Some students may benefit from further support with sentence starters, such as:

  ◊ History: The first mobile phones appeared in the 1980s…
  ◊ What they can do: Mobile phones are far more than 'phones'…
  ◊ Types of phones: The highest levels of technology in a smartphone mean that… If you just want to make a call, pay-as-you-go phones…

# Unit focus

## Preparation and resources

- Student Book 1: pages p76–81
- Workbook 1: pages 26–27
- Kerboodle resources:
  ◇ 3.2 Mary Anning, discoverer of prehistoric fossils audio
  ◇ 3.2 Mary Anning, discoverer of prehistoric fossils quiz
  ◇ 3.2 Word power worksheet
  ◇ 3.2 Combining information worksheet
- Grammatical knowledge: phrase
- Key terms: biographical dictionary (WB), biography, chronological (WB), context, phrase, scanning (WB)

## What this unit teaches and how

- The webpage extract, 'Mary Anning, discoverer of prehistoric fossils' is a summarised series of biographical facts about the life and work of Mary Anning. Students are asked to find key information from different parts of the text. They are also asked to combine information in their own writing.

- *Catapult Workbook 1* supports and develops the skills in this unit further through an account of the life of Charles Darwin from *A Short Biographical Dictionary of English Literature*. Students develop their understanding of archaic language and develop their skills to locate relevant information and write it down in chronological order.

## Skills and objectives

In this unit, students will:

- Find relevant information from different parts of a text.

- Combine information to develop and demonstrate overall understanding.

- Learn, understand and practise using new vocabulary.

# Teaching suggestions and guidance

This unit is designed to cover two to three lessons, depending on the ability level of your students and the length of lesson time.

### Introduction to the unit (p76)

- Ask groups to discuss inspirational people and what they have achieved. This could be divided into people from history and people from more recent times (including family members). Gather ideas from the groups. Focus on those people who have inspired others by what they have managed to do 'against the odds'.

- Ask students what they understand by the word 'biography'. Point out that 'bio' is from a Greek word meaning 'life'. Draw out that a biography is the story of someone's life, written by someone else. Discuss how an autobiography differs (it is written by the subject themselves; the prefix 'auto' means self).

### Engaging with the source text (p77)

- Ask students to prepare a reading of different sections of the text in pairs, then share the readings as a class. Project a picture of Mary Anning on the IWB during the reading. Alternatively, play the audio recording of the text on Kerboodle: 3.2 Mary Anning, discoverer of prehistoric fossils audio.

- Take feedback on the 'Ready, set, go!' task in the Student Book, drawing out the variety of information from the perspective of a life summary, anecdote and factfile.

- To test basic comprehension of the extract, ask students to complete the 3.2 Mary Anning, discoverer of prehistoric fossils quiz on Kerboodle. This can be completed either individually or as a whole-class activity.

**Resources**
◇ Kerboodle: 3.2 Mary Anning, discoverer of prehistoric fossils audio
◇ Kerboodle: 3.2 Mary Anning, discoverer of prehistoric fossils quiz

## Word power (pp78–79)

- For Activity 2, if students need more support, guide them towards the following people:

  ◇ Sport: Roger Bannister – the first person to run a mile in under 4 minutes; Jessica Ennis-Hill – Olympic and World champion at the Heptathlon.
  ◇ Music: The Beatles – the first group to sell millions of records that introduced many new styles of music to the public.
  ◇ Science: Tim Berners-Lee – inventor of the Internet; Rosalind Franklin – part of the team who discovered DNA.

- Encourage students to use the 3.2 Word power worksheet on Kerboodle to help reinforce their understanding of the target words in this unit.

**Resources**
◇ Kerboodle: 3.2 Word power worksheet

## Knowledge and understanding (p80)

- The activities in this section will develop students' abilities to find relevant information from the whole text. Depending on ability range, you may wish to focus students on the relevant part of the text for each activity.

- Alternatively, the questions could be dealt with in teams of equal ability spread, with a set time given for each question. The answers can be gathered in a quiz format before the actual answers are revealed.

## Reading skills (pp80–81)

- In this section, students are asked to combine the information they have learned in order to make wider assumptions. Model this by giving examples based on current events or news, e.g. Given… and…, what can we learn about…?

- Use the 3.2 Combining information worksheet on Kerboodle to help students practise the skill of drawing information from more than one source in order to inform their own writing.

- For Activity 4, some students might benefit from some sentence starters, such as:

  ◇ Her determination meant that…
  ◇ She must have been very dependable because…
  ◇ If you could go back in time and meet her, she would…

Ensure students support what they say by referring very closely to the text, using either direct quotations or paraphrasing.

**Resources**
◇ Kerboodle: 3.2 Combining information worksheet

## Check your skills (p81)

- The final section asks students to look at what they understand about the wider picture of 19th-century life. In addition to the sentence starters, support students with vocabulary for part (a):

  ◇ Attitudes to science: amateur, prejudiced, exclusive
  ◇ Attitudes to women: dismissive, patronising
  ◇ Poverty and wealth: unfair, uncaring
  ◇ Health: multiple births, safety hats, mortality rates.

- Students could collaborate after writing and create a presentation about Mary Anning and why she is so famous.

# Unit focus

## Preparation and resources

- Student Book 1: pages 82–87
- Workbook 1: pages 28–29
- Kerboodle resources:
  - 3.3 Delivery robots audio
  - 3.3 Delivery robots quiz
  - 3.3 Word power worksheet
  - 3.3 Implied meaning worksheet
- Grammatical knowledge: clause, conjunction, modal verb, multi-clause sentence, second-person pronoun
- Key terms: clause, conjunction, imperative (WB), modal verb, multi-clause sentence, second-person pronoun, sentence structure, verb (WB)

## What this unit teaches and how

- The webpage text, 'Delivery robots to replace takeaway drivers in London trial' is used as a stimulus to analyse language and presentation of information in a news report. Students put their learning into practice by writing their own article about new technology.

- *Catapult Workbook 1* supports and develops the skills in this unit through analysing aspects of a news report from 1958, 'Meet the one-eyed robot – it's fantastic'. There is particular focus on analysis of sentence structure and effective headlines and openings.

## Skills and objectives

In this unit, students will:

- Understand how a writer uses sentence structure and paragraphs to make information interesting and relevant to the reader.

- Practise writing their own informative and relevant news report.

- Learn, understand and practise using new vocabulary.

# Teaching suggestions and guidance

This unit is designed to cover two to three lessons, depending on the ability level of your students and the length of lesson time.

## Introduction to the unit (p82)

- Discuss the way that technology has changed people's lives over the last few decades. Ask students to identify five changes to our lives that have been the consequence of new technology (perhaps focus on the effects of mobile phones, computers and the Internet). Steer students to a consensus that technology supports our daily life but can have detrimental effects too (e.g. an addiction to social media).

- Ask students to pick a use of technology in their lives and find a way to complete the sentence: '… is an essential part of my life because…'.

## Engaging with the source text (p83)

- Ask students in groups to consider how technology could possibly improve the delivery of fast food. Share ideas – some students may already have heard about the subject of the text.

- Read the text with students. Alternatively, play the audio recording of the extract on Kerboodle: 3.3 Delivery robots audio.

- Take feedback in response to the 'Ready, set, go!' task in the Student Book. Draw out that quotations add human interest to a story, can act as witnesses to confirm facts and can supply additional information.

- To test basic comprehension of the extract, ask students to complete the 3.3 Delivery robots quiz on Kerboodle. This can be completed either individually or as a whole-class activity.

**Resources**

- Kerboodle: 3.3 Delivery robots audio
- Kerboodle: 3.3 Delivery robots quiz

## Word power (pp84–85)

- Target words are also listed in the target word list at the back of the Student Book so encourage students to access this if necessary.

- For Activity 4, ask students to use an appropriate adverb with 'unfazed' to amplify the effect of the word (e.g. strangely, unusually, weirdly).

- Activity 5 asks students to write about an unplanned meeting with a delivery robot in their local high street. Set a limit of 50 words for the task. Suggest some appropriate stylistic features such as imagery to help make the description memorable, e.g.

  ◇ It was like watching an alien invasion as…
  ◇ People jumped out of the way as if it was an escaped wild animal and…

- Share examples of students' writing with the whole class. Encourage students to try and reflect on the shock at seeing something so unusual.

- Use the 3.3 Word power worksheet on Kerboodle to help reinforce students' understanding of prefixes and compound words.

**Resource**
◇ Kerboodle: 3.3 Word power worksheet

## Knowledge and understanding (p85)

- For Activity 1, students could be given copies of the text so they can highlight five discrete things we learn about the delivery robots. Share the facts and ensure that all selected details are facts.

- Use the 3.3 Implied meaning worksheet on Kerboodle to explore and reinforce students' understanding of this concept.

- For Activity 5, some students might benefit from being given a sentence starter, such as:

  ◇ The quotation points out that…

- As an additional question, ask students why they think that the quotation beginning, 'Kids love it' has been placed at the end of the text. Draw out responses such as: for humour; to show that if children accept them, so should adults, i.e. they are harmless.

**Resource**
◇ Kerboodle: 3.3 Implied meaning worksheet

## Writing skills (pp86–87)

- This section begins by explaining the grammatical structure of the first sentence in the article. Demonstrate other examples using the following sentences:

  ◇ You might enjoy going to the local park.
  ◇ You should be careful when choosing where to go shopping.

  Ask students to highlight relevant parts to ensure that the principles are understood.

- For Activity 3, support students with ideas for who might be quoted, e.g. the inventor, a marketing manager, a disability rights campaigner.

- For Activity 4, give students further ideas for the information that could be included in their next paragraph, e.g. the benefits for disabled people.

## Check your skills (p87)

- If some students require more support in this writing task, guide them towards sentences such as:

  ◇ Your lives will be so much easier with the voice-activated TV – you will not regret bringing one into your home!
  ◇ What has been missing in your life? That's right, a voice-activated TV!
  ◇ We are convinced that this will improve everyone's lives.
  ◇ Life will never be the same again. We are excited by our invention and hope that you will feel the same!

- Students could use a partner to peer-assess and look for implementation of the features and the accuracy of the writing. The latter might include spelling, punctuation and correct grammar.

# Unit focus

## Preparation and resources

- Student Book 1: pages 88–93
- Workbook 1: pages 30–31
- Kerboodle resources:
  ◇ 3.4 All About the Telephone and Phonograph audio
  ◇ 3.4 All About the Telephone and Phonograph quiz
  ◇ 3.4 Word power worksheet
  ◇ 3.4 Main clauses worksheet
- Grammatical knowledge: main clause, passive voice
- Key terms: active voice (WB), main clause, novel, passive voice, tone

## What this unit teaches and how

- The text, *All About the Telephone and Phonograph*, written in 1878, reflects an awe-struck response to the technological advances of the time, i.e. the telegraph, the telephone and the phonograph. The unit explores the common 19th-century style of multi-clause sentences and how the tone of the writer is conveyed.

- *Catapult Workbook 1* supports and develops the skills in this lesson with further analysis of another 19th-century text, 'The Making of a Tunnel – the Waterloo and City Railway' (1895). Activities focus in particular on the use of the passive and active voice.

## Skills and objectives

In this unit, students will:

- Gather information from a 19th-century text.

- Understand how sentence forms, punctuation and language choices are used to communicate meaning and tone in a 19th-century text.

- Learn, understand and practise using new vocabulary.

# Teaching suggestions and guidance

This unit is designed to cover two to three lessons, depending on the ability level of your students and the length of lesson time.

## Introduction to the unit (p88)

- Display pictures of 19th-century advertisements for the technological wonders of the time, e.g. typewriters, showers, cameras. Discuss when these products were first invented and available to the consumer (typewriters 1865, home showers 1880s, camera 1888). Use the development of the home computer to bring perspective (generally firstly available at great cost in the early 1980s).

- Ensure that students realise that technological progress made in the 19th-century world was just as rapid as today, although we take those 'inventions' for granted nowadays.

## Engaging with the source text (p89)

- Read the text with students in a tone that reflects the amazement of the writer. Alternatively, play the audio recording of the extract on Kerboodle: 3.4 All About the Telephone and Phonograph audio.

- Ask students to consider what changes the inventions described in the text made to people's lives. Draw out the increase in the speed of communication over distances.

- Take feedback from students on the 'Ready, set, go!' task. Draw out that the writer describes in great detail how the sound of the human voice can be transmitted by telephone and even recorded onto a plate that can be sent by post and replayed by the receiving person.

- To test basic comprehension of *All About the Telephone and Phonograph*, ask students to complete the 3.4 All About the Telephone and Phonograph quiz on Kerboodle. This can be completed either individually or as a whole-class activity.

## Resources
◇ Kerboodle: 3.4 All About the Telephone and Phonograph audio
◇ Kerboodle: 3.4 All About the Telephone and Phonograph quiz

## Word power (pp90-91)

- For Activity 3, most students will offer 'command of the language/of French' as their answer. You may want to mention that the phrase 'command of' could also refer to finance or an organisation. For example:

  ◇ I have a good command of maths and can calculate quickly.
  ◇ She has a good command of the way things work in the organisation and can get things done.

- For Activity 5, support students with the following sentence starters:

  ◇ I cannot stress enough just how miraculous…
  ◇ The world has completely changed from today because…
  ◇ Prepare yourselves for wonders beyond the imagination…

- Use the 3.4 Word power worksheet on Kerboodle to help secure students' confidence in using the target vocabulary from the Student Book in more familiar and modern contexts. This worksheet also reinforces understanding of the passive voice.

### Resource
◇ Kerboodle: 3.4 Word power worksheet

## Knowledge and understanding (p91)

- The questions in this section can be dealt with quickly through pair work, group discussion or a quiz format with a choice of answers.

- Ensure that students explain their answers to Activities 3 and 4 using full sentences. If they need prompting, encourage them to describe what the writer 'does' using terms such as: explains, describes, states.

## Reading skills (pp92-93)

- This section helps students to understand the complexities of the sentence structure of this 19th-century text through looking at the relatively brief main clause and the lengthy detail added in the middle of it.

- Students may need to be supported with the final part of Activity 1. Remind them that the main clause is the part of the sentence that makes sense on its own and is not dependent on any other parts to make its meaning clear.

- For Activity 2a, students could work in pairs or the information gathering could be done as a whole group with students writing information on the IWB.

- For Activity 3, when students have identified the word 'excited', ask them to think of other words that would describe the tone and convey a similar meaning (e.g. enthusiastic).

- Use 3.4 Main clauses worksheet on Kerboodle to reinforce students' understanding of clauses.

### Resource
◇ Kerboodle: 3.4 Main clauses worksheet

## Check your skills (p93)

- The final task allows students to gather together lots of information learned from the text in order to explain the writer's attitude towards the new technology.

- Some students may benefit from support in finding evidence for their ideas in the text. Remind them how to include short quotations or to paraphrase the text.

- If necessary, exemplify the way the sections may be written by offering some sentence starters, such as:

  ◇ The reader cannot fail to notice the excitement of the writer as…
  ◇ The detailed descriptions of the inventions show that…
  ◇ The writer is optimistic about the future because he states that we should…

# Assessment suggestions and guidance

## Why are we assessing this?

Students have completed the chapter on Explanations and insights, exploring a variety of high-quality contemporary, 20th- and pre-20th-century non-fiction texts. The units have reinforced and developed the essential reading and writing skills outlined below, consolidating knowledge and increasing students' confidence.

This assessment unit gives students and teachers the opportunity to assess and reflect on how firmly these skills – in particular, the reading skills – have been grasped and how effectively students can employ them in an assessment situation.

## What are students demonstrating?

Students are asked to:

- identify key information
- analyse how a writer uses language to convey meaning and tone
- combine information to develop and demonstrate overall understanding.

## How to deliver the assessment

- You may wish to break down the assessment unit into individual activities, particularly with students who still find the development of text analysis challenging. Success in shorter activities will help to instil the confidence needed to achieve or move closer to learning targets.
- Where appropriate, students may be supported by allowing time to discuss what is expected in the assessment activities. This could be done for the assessment as a whole or on a question-by-question basis.
- For more confident students, the assessment can be used in its entirety, to be completed under exam-type conditions within a set time limit.
- The reading assessment is based on two texts about Ada Byron Lovelace. They are accessible texts for most readers, but you may wish to read them aloud during the assessment and even

re-read extracts linked to particular questions to support students further. Audio recordings of the extracts are available on Kerboodle: 3.5 The world's first computer programmer (1815–1852) audio and 3.5 Ada Lovelace fact file audio.

## How to mark the assessment

You will want to mark this in line with departmental and school marking guidelines. If you wish, you could use the *Catapult* marking scales (provided on Kerboodle). The *Catapult* marking scales are designed to assess lower-attaining students who need to consolidate skills that have not yet been fully grasped but need to be secured and developed in order to move those students forward and narrow the gap between their existing levels of achievement and national expectations for KS3.

Using the *Catapult* marking scales will help you to identify specific strengths and areas for improvement in an individual student's reading. This may help you to set development targets as well as build a profile of your class as readers.

## Following up the assessment

The assessment should enable you to identify clear areas in which students have underperformed and you can therefore plan in detail how to reinforce understanding using *Catapult* resources.

1. Refer to the *Catapult* mapping grids on pages 132-135 of this Teacher Book to identify other *Catapult* chapters where these reading and writing skills are covered. For example:

   ◊ identifying key information from the text is also covered in Chapter 5 (Units 3 and 4) and Chapter 6 (Unit 2).

2. Direct students to the SPaG quizzes on Kerboodle to address any areas of weakness that the assessment may have revealed. For example, basic skills can be reinforced with the following quizzes:

   ◊ Capital letters
   ◊ Full stops
   ◊ Commas
   ◊ Common and proper nouns
   ◊ Sentences
   ◊ Clauses
   ◊ Active and passive voice.

Encourage students to proofread their work, looking for ways of making their writing style more concise and fluent. For example, skills can be reinforced with the following quizzes:

⬦ Noun phrases
⬦ Adverbials
⬦ Adjectives
⬦ Adverbs
⬦ Conjunctions
⬦ Parenthesis
⬦ Verbs and tenses.

The Grammar reference guide on Kerboodle contains definitions and additional examples of each of the spelling, punctuation and grammar points covered in the quizzes, for your reference.

3. If students' vocabulary seems limited, remind them to make use of the target words they have explored, which are also contained in the target word list at the back of the Student Book. Students may also benefit from compiling their own vocabulary lists for reference. These should be shared and discussed regularly.

4. Work with students to increase their confidence in spelling key grammatical and literary terms, e.g. preposition, conjunction, quotation, synonym, adverbial, sentence, exclamation, simile, metaphor, personification. Lower-attaining students may resist using these terms in their writing if they are unsure of spellings, even if they understand the meaning.

5. Ensure students are competent at spelling high-frequency words, particularly those that are commonly misspelt, e.g. people, because, family, its/it's, across, achieve, believe, coming, completely, sentence, finally, friend, immediately, separate, remember, truly, surprise, weird, fortunately, therefore, successful, tomorrow. Encourage strategies to learn these spellings, using mnemonics, chanting, singing, repetition and any other ways that help to embed the knowledge.

### Resources
⬦ Kerboodle: *Catapult* marking scales
⬦ Kerboodle: SPaG quizzes
⬦ Kerboodle: Grammar reference guide

Note that the source texts and activities in *Catapult Workbook 1* can also be used as assessment material, if students haven't already used them to consolidate their learning from the Student Book.

# Chapter 4:
# Opinion and persuasion

## Chapter overview

### Why are we teaching this?

Understanding how writers present opinions, and seek to persuade others to agree with them, is an important aspect of critical appreciation of non-fiction. By exploring high-quality texts and focusing on particular persuasive techniques that writers use, students can then develop their own writing through carefully supported activities.

Across the four units in this chapter, students will read a variety of texts that present opinions. The texts include a speech by 13-year-old Severn Suzuki, given to a UN conference, a letter to a national newspaper about wheelchair users, and an extract from a campaign website encouraging parents to allow their children to play outside. Students are given the opportunity to use the skills and techniques they have studied in these extracts in the writing assessment at the end of the chapter.

Although most of the activities in this chapter will produce written outcomes, many will benefit from prior discussion. Some activities could be adapted to oral activities. Ensure students are aware of the link between persuasive speeches and texts, and how they use similar techniques.

### What are the learning aims?

In every unit in this chapter, students will learn to strengthen the core skills of:

- vocabulary
- increasing general knowledge and contextual understanding.

In addition, units will focus on the following learning aims. Students will:

| Unit 1 | Unit 2 | Unit 3 | Unit 4 |
|---|---|---|---|
| • Explore how text structure and sentence structure can be used to persuade an audience.<br>• Use these features to make their own writing more effective.<br>• Learn, understand and practise using new vocabulary. | • Explore how a writer uses language and structure to communicate strong emotions in a persuasive text.<br>• Explore how a writer uses contrast to persuade an audience.<br>• Learn, understand and practise using new vocabulary. | • Explore how a writer varies verb tenses to create specific effects.<br>• Create an effective opening and ending to a letter, using paragraphs to structure their ideas.<br>• Learn, understand and practise using new vocabulary. | • Make inferences, using evidence from the text to support their ideas.<br>• Read closely to analyse how a writer uses language, and selects and contrasts information, to persuade.<br>• Learn, understand and practise using new vocabulary. |

### How will this chapter be assessed?

The writing assessment at the end of the chapter gives students three different tasks for writing based on the skills practised through the units. There is clear guidance for planning with suggested criteria for inclusion in each piece.

The focuses for assessment will be persuasive techniques:

- lists to give examples and emphasis
- repetition to provide rhythm and make memorable patterns
- personal experience
- language chosen to make the reader feel a particular emotion (e.g. anger, empathy)
- pronouns to include the reader (we) and to address the reader (you)
- contrast of images and ideas
- use of past and present tense to urge the need for action
- verbs, adjectives and adverbs chosen for effect
- rhetorical questions for dramatic effect.

These focuses for assessment may vary in emphasis depending on the writing task that students complete.

Note that the short 'Check your skills' feature at the end of every unit in this chapter provides formative assessment opportunities to support students' learning.

## Chapter 4 unit sequence

The sequence of units is designed so that students gain in confidence as they complete more challenging activities while progressing through the chapter.

Note that some activities feature in just the Teacher Book (TB).

| Chapter 4: Opinion and persuasion | | |
|---|---|---|
| | Student Book | Workbook |
| **1: A call for change** | **Source text:** Extract 1 from Severn Suzuki's speech<br><br>• Discuss the issue of damage to the environment by human activity. (TB)<br>• Analyse why the opening of the speech is effective and explore the grouping of information.<br>• Write an additional paragraph for the speech. | **Source text:** Extract from Barack Obama speech<br><br>• Identify use of repetition, emotive language, 'list of three' and inclusive pronouns.<br>• Write an analysis of the speech. |
| **2: Encouraging action** | **Source text:** Extract 2 from Severn Suzuki's speech<br><br>• Discuss which environmental issues are the most critical and invite ideas for action. (TB)<br>• Reflect on the development of the speech and its impact.<br>• Explore the effect of rhythm, emotive language and rhetorical questions.<br>• Write an explanation of why the speech can evoke anger. | **Source text:** Extract from Henry V's speech<br><br>• Analyse rhythm, comparisons and emotive language.<br>• Write a short persuasive speech. |
| **3: Speaking from experience** | **Source text:** Letter to a newspaper: 'Please stop treating wheelchair users as if they are invisible'<br><br>• Consider the school's accessibility for wheelchair users. (TB)<br>• Explore the structural features of the letter.<br>• Write a letter to persuade an audience of shopkeepers that they are discriminating against children. | **Source text:** Extract from *I was a bully*<br><br>• Identify colloquial language and the effects of verb tenses.<br>• Create a personal account using techniques explored in the source text. |

<table>
<tr><td colspan="3" align="center">Chapter 4:<br>Opinion and persuasion</td></tr>
</table>

| | Student Book | Workbook |
|---|---|---|
| **4: Support our campaign** | **Source text:** Extract from 'Playing Out' website<br><br>• Discuss students' experiences of play as children and compare with different generations. (TB)<br>• Analyse the use of language designed to persuade the reader, the selection of memories to appeal to the reader, and the contrasts drawn out between different generations.<br>• Write an analysis of how the writer has used particular effects to persuade a reader of the argument for more unstructured play. | **Source text:** Extract from Plastic Pollution Coalition website<br><br>• Identify effective phrases and imagery.<br>• Insert relevant quotations into a written response. |
| **Writing assessment** | **Task:** select one of three writing tasks about promoting more outdoor facilities for children's play<br><br>• Advice about planning, writing and editing a first draft.<br>• Criteria for the persuasive techniques expected to be demonstrated in the writing. | |

# Preparing to teach

## Refresh your knowledge

You might find it helpful to refer to the following key points when planning the teaching of this chapter:

• The classic art of rhetoric (public speaking in order to persuade people) was developed during the emergence of democracy in Athens in about 460 BC, when politicians needed to master the art of public speaking in order to participate in assemblies and councils, and people from many different levels of society wanted to be able to put forward their viewpoints in law courts and local debates. Artistotle's famous collection of notes, *Art of Rhetoric*, gives detailed guidance on the principles of oratorical skill, which are still used by speakers today.

• Being able to influence people through speech or writing is a great power in all aspects of life, whether in politics, business, the media or simply among friends and family. Many great speeches or persuasive writings have marked a turning point in history or created a huge mind-shift in people's beliefs or understanding. Persuasive language can lead to change; it is a way of galvanising support for a cause, an ideal, a group or an individual person.

• Many persuasive devices used in speeches are also employed effectively in writing when the writer wants to persuade readers to their viewpoint or to take action. Persuasive writing can be found in many places, such as campaign leaflets, letters of protest, political manifestos and charity appeals.

## Links and further reading

• The following link gives more advice on persuasive strategies (e.g. repetition, reasons why, consistency, social proof, comparisons, etc.): https://www.copyblogger.com/persuasive-writing/. Originally written to advise copywriters on timeless techniques, it offers more detailed background on persuasive writing for teachers.

- A film of the original speech by Severn Suzuki, with images to illustrate the subject and an extract of the adult Severn still making her point and enthusing the young, can be found at the following link: https://www.youtube.com/watch?v=3ipOdsd1SmA.
- Severn Suzuki's book, *Tell the World*, was written for school students in 1993. It expands on the issues covered in the speech and students will find it interesting to see if anything has changed.
- Further advice for students about writing persuasive letters can be found on numerous websites. For GCSE Bitesize, follow the link at: http://www.bbc.co.uk/schools/gcsebitesize/english/writing/genreaudiencerev4.shtml.
- There are numerous websites devoted to the views and perspectives of wheelchair users. 'New Mobility – Life Beyond Wheels' can be found at: http://www.newmobility.com/2016/04/global-perspectives/. This site gives a global perspective and shares the experiences of wheelchair users in countries such as Croatia and the Ukraine.
- Students could be guided to novels that evoke the freedom of the past, when children could play and explore without the interruption of adults, such as *Swallows and Amazons* by Arthur Ransome. Sections of *Kes*, where Billy Casper is walking in the woods and escaping his urban poverty, are particularly powerful in evoking a sense of wonder with the natural world.
- Jon Henley has written in *The Guardian* about the benefits of ensuring that children have the opportunity to play in the natural environment and will give you further subject matter to use in the lesson: https://www.theguardian.com/lifeandstyle/2010/aug/16/childre-nature-outside-play-health.
- The Council for Learning Outside the Classroom has an advice sheet at the following link: http://www.lotc.org.uk/wp-content/uploads/2010/12/Benefits-for-Early-Years-LOtC-Final-5AUG09.pdf.

## Planning guidance and teaching tips

Think about how you can make the materials relevant to your students and responsive to their particular needs and learning targets. Some suggested approaches to address key areas are provided below.

- Encourage wider reading wherever possible, particularly in relation to different persuasive texts. Also encourage listening to or reading speeches, e.g. those made at political or campaign rallies. Ask students to try to identify persuasive techniques they have learned about in this chapter.
- All the target words are in the target word list at the back of the Student Book. Encourage students to use this to establish the habit of looking up words as part of the process of discussing and exploring their meaning.
- The texts studied in this chapter are not too lexically challenging. However, students will learn that language is not just about the use of particular vocabulary. The key to effective persuasion is often through the repetition of sentence structures and the switching of perspectives from the speaker/writer to the listener/reader to evoke empathy and a sense of responsibility.
- All the texts in this chapter of the Student Book and the Workbook have a definite purpose, whether it is to raise awareness of the damage humans have done to the environment, to instil loyalty in troops, or to express shock at the treatment of someone with a disability. When writing their own persuasive texts, students need to have a firm grasp of the purpose of the text before they undertake detailed planning and preparation. If the purpose is not properly grasped, the text will not be effective.
- Refer to the Grammar reference guide on Kerboodle for definitions and exemplars of specific grammar and punctuation terms covered in this chapter. Kerboodle also provides quizzes to help improve the technical accuracy of students' writing and the application of grammar in context.

# Unit focus

## Preparation and resources

- Student Book 1: pages 96–101
- Workbook 1: pages 32–33
- Kerboodle resources:
  - ◇ 4.1 Severn Suzuki's speech extract 1 audio
  - ◇ 4.1 Severn Suzuki's speech extract 1 quiz
  - ◇ 4.1 Word power worksheet
  - ◇ 4.1 Lists and groups of three worksheet
- Grammatical knowledge: phrase
- Key terms: context, emotive language (WB), inclusive pronoun (WB), phrase, sentence structure, structure, summary

## What this unit teaches and how

- The extract from Severn Suzuki's speech is a powerful indictment of what the speaker sees as the damage caused by adults to the world she will inherit. The text of the speech is analysed for the way it builds a strong persuasive case through the use of direct address, lists and a strong structure based on key questions.

- *Catapult Workbook 1* supports and develops the skills in this unit through a short extract from a speech made by Barack Obama about the need to combat climate change. Students are led through activities that explore the persuasive qualities of the language and delivery of the speech.

## Skills and objectives

In this unit, students will:

- Explore how text structure and sentence structure can be used to persuade an audience.

- Use these features to make their own writing more effective.

- Learn, understand and practise using new vocabulary.

# Teaching suggestions and guidance

This unit is designed to cover two to three lessons, depending on the ability level of your students and the length of lesson time.

## Introduction to the unit (p96)

- Ask students to work in pairs to discuss what they think are the most important issues relating to environmental damage. Encourage them to gather vocabulary linked to the subject.

- Take feedback to share understanding of the threats to the environment. Topics might include plastic pollution, global warming, rainforest clearance and destruction of natural habitats for wildlife. Note specific vocabulary related to these issues and also to students' personal responses to them, e.g. worried, anxious, protective.

## Engaging with the source text (p97)

- Practise reading the speech so that the persuasive drama is emphasised. Alternatively, play the original televised clip of the speech at: https://www.youtube.com/watch?v=oJJGuIZVfLM or play the audio recording of the extract on Kerboodle: 4.1 Severn Suzuki's speech extract 1 audio.

- Take feedback on the 'Ready, set, go!' task. Draw out that Suzuki felt she was representing all starving children, dying animals and generations to come. She was speaking to delegates and reporters at the conference and, through them, to all adults.

- To test basic comprehension of the extract, ask students to complete the 4.1 Severn Suzuki's speech extract 1 quiz on Kerboodle. This can be completed as a whole-class activity or individually.

### Resources
- ◇ Kerboodle: 4.1 Severn Suzuki's speech extract 1 audio
- ◇ Kerboodle: 4.1 Severn Suzuki's speech extract 1 quiz

## Word power (pp98–99)

- Students could work individually on Activities 1–4, then share answers as a whole-class activity.

- For Activity 2, ensure students' understanding of the concept of context is secure. If necessary, explain that a fish's natural context is in water. This visual, literal image may help students to grasp the concept.

- In Activity 5, give a word limit for the summary of no more than 25 words. Share the summaries once complete, praising the most concise.

- Use the 4.1 Word power worksheet on Kerboodle to reinforce students' confidence with the vocabulary in this unit.

**Resources**
◇ Kerboodle: 4.1 Word power worksheet

## Knowledge and understanding (p99)

- Encourage students to explain their answers to Activities 2 and 3 with close reference to the text.

- In Activity 4, remind students that the use of the second-person pronoun 'you' makes clear the difference between the speaker and the audience (or writer and reader).

## Writing skills (pp100–101)

- Students could complete Activity 1 in pairs, then share their ideas with the whole class.

- For Activity 2, guide students towards thinking about imagery created by the phrases 'herds of wild animals', 'jungles' and 'rainforests full of birds and butterflies'. Point out that a description such as 'rainforests full of insects and snakes' might not have been so effective.

- In responding to Activity 3b, remind students that this speech was given in 1992. Ask them whether they think the effect of the speech on them is any different to the effect on the original audience. Is the speech still relevant?

- Use the 4.1 Lists and groups of three worksheet on Kerboodle to develop and reinforce students' understanding of listing and its effects.

**Resources**
◇ Kerboodle: 4.1 Lists and groups of three worksheet

## Check your skills (p101)

- Students are asked to write an additional paragraph for the speech. Ensure they understand that they can use the information in the panel headed 'The effects of climate change'.

- To support students, offer the following sentence starters:

  ◇ If the Earth could speak, it would tell you that…
  ◇ You have a duty to go away and…
  ◇ Just like me, your children will inherit what is left of…

- Students could peer-assess each other's first drafts, using the bullet points as a checklist, before writing a final draft.

# Unit focus

## Preparation and resources

- Student Book 1: pages 102–107
- Workbook 1: pages 34–35
- Kerboodle resources:
  ◇ 4.2 Severn Suzuki's speech extract 2 audio
  ◇ 4.2 Severn Suzuki's speech extract 2 quiz
  ◇ 4.2 Word power worksheet
  ◇ 4.2 Commenting on emotional language worksheet
- Key terms: alliteration (WB), contrast, imperative (WB), rhetorical question, rhythm, verb (WB)

## What this unit teaches and how

- The second extract from Severn Suzuki's speech takes students through to the end of her warning to the world. The activities in this unit focus on the effects of generating rhythm in the speech, rhetorical questions and emotional language.

- *Catapult Workbook 1* supports and develops the skills in this unit further through analysing a speech from *Henry V* by William Shakespeare. The speech by King Henry is designed to enthuse his troops before battle, stirring up their emotions and appetite for confrontation.

## Skills and objectives

In this unit, students will:

- Explore how a writer uses language and structure to communicate strong emotions in a persuasive text.

- Explore how a writer uses contrast to persuade an audience.

- Learn, understand and practise using new vocabulary.

# Teaching suggestions and guidance

This unit is designed to cover two to three lessons, depending on the ability level of your students and the length of lesson time.

## Introduction to the unit (p102)

- Remind students of the environmental issues they identified in the previous unit. Ask them which issues they feel are most urgent and encourage them to suggest action that should be taken to address them.

- Ask students who they think should drive changes to combat environmental damage: governments, businesses, individuals, or a mix. Encourage them to explain their reasons carefully.

## Engaging with the source text (p103)

- You could use the original televised clip of the speech (the extract begins at 2m 59s) at: https://www.youtube.com/watch?v=oJJGuIZVfLM. Alternatively, play the audio recording of the extract on Kerboodle: 4.2 Severn Suzuki's speech extract 2 audio.

- Take feedback from the 'Ready, set, go!' task. Ensure students draw out the contrasting lifestyles in Canada and Brazil described in the third paragraph of the source text.

- To test basic comprehension of the extract, ask students to complete the 4.2 Severn Suzuki's speech extract 2 quiz on Kerboodle. This can be completed as a whole-class activity or individually.

### Resources
◇ Kerboodle: 4.2 Severn Suzuki's speech extract 2 audio
◇ Kerboodle: 4.2 Severn Suzuki's speech extract 2 quiz

## Word power (pp104–105)

- In Activity 2, ask students what they consider to be the main privilege of living in a wealthy and prosperous country. Draw out thoughts about education, healthcare and public provision of water and sanitation, a peaceful society, etc. Ensure students think beyond material wealth.

- If students need more support for Activity 4, it could be simplified by asking them to end the sentence:

  ◊ A global solution to environmental problems is important because…

- Use the 4.2 Word power worksheet on Kerboodle to reinforce students' understanding of the vocabulary in the source text, through the use of synonyms.

**Resources**
◊ Kerboodle: 4.2 Word power worksheet

## Knowledge and understanding (p105)

- For Activity 1, ask students how the image of a family strengthens Suzuki's argument.

- For Activity 2b, encourage students to explain their choice of word with close reference to the source text.

- If students need more guidance for Activity 4, remind them of the word 'privilege'.

## Reading skills (pp106–107)

- Ensure students appreciate the repetition in the sound and structure of the highlighted text. Link this pattern of sound with their understanding of rhythm in music.

- If necessary, before tackling Activity 2, refresh students' knowledge of rhetorical questions, giving other examples that are commonly used, such as 'What can I say?', 'How can I keep quiet?', 'Didn't you hear what I said?' Remind them that rhetorical questions don't expect an actual response, but they challenge the audience/reader to think about something.

- Use the 4.2 Commenting on emotional language worksheet on Kerboodle to develop students' skills in comprehending and commenting on emotional word choice in texts.

**Resources**
◊ Kerboodle: 4.2 Commenting on emotional language worksheet

## Check your skills (p107)

- Draw attention to the caption on page 107. Ensure students understand the reference to 'Plan A/B' and the link to the word 'planet'. Ask what the poster is implying. Draw out that we have no alternative but to sort out this one planet that we have.

- This final section focuses on the impact of the speech outside the original audience in 1992. Students should have plenty of material to use as evidence for why a young person today may feel angry after reading the speech. Ask whether they have cause to be more angry than 25 years ago.

- Use the following sentence starters to support students' writing:

  ◊ The power of Suzuki's argument manages to…
  ◊ The issues explored in the speech…
  ◊ When young people read this speech, they are bound to feel angry because…
  ◊ Suzuki wants young people to be angry because…

# Unit focus

## Preparation and resources

- Student Book 1: pages 108–113
- Workbook 1: pages 36–37
- Kerboodle resources:
  ◇ 4.3 Wheelchair users audio
  ◇ 4.3 Wheelchair users quiz
  ◇ 4.3 Word power worksheet
  ◇ 4.3 Inclusive language worksheet
- Grammatical knowledge: past tense, present tense, pronoun
- Key terms: conclusion, contraction (WB), formal language (WB), imply, informal language, past tense, present tense, pronoun, verb tenses

## What this unit teaches and how

- This unit focuses on a letter written to a national newspaper about the way the writer's wife was treated while having to use a wheelchair. Activities focus on how the vocabulary, structure and use of pronouns develop the persuasive effect of the text. Students are given opportunities to use these techniques in their own writing.

- *Catapult Workbook 1* supports and develops the skills in this unit further through the article *I was a bully*. This recounts a regretted incident from the writer's youth and he tries to dissuade readers from making the same mistakes.

## Skills and objectives

In this unit, students will:

- Explore how a writer varies verb tenses to create specific effects.

- Create an effective opening and ending to a letter, using paragraphs to structure their ideas.

- Learn, understand and practise using new vocabulary.

# Teaching suggestions and guidance

This unit is designed to cover two to three lessons, depending on the ability level of your students and the length of lesson time.

## Introduction to the unit (p108)

Note that sensitivity should be exercised throughout this unit if there are any students in the class who have a disability.

- Ask students whether they think that the needs of people with disabilities are taken into consideration as much as they should be.

- Students could consider the way that someone in a wheelchair can manoeuvre round their own site and school building. Perhaps some students already do. Is anywhere inaccessible? Rate the positive and negative disability-access aspects of the school.

## Engaging with the source text (p109)

- Read the text in a voice that reflects the writer's reasonable character but shock at the treatment faced by his wife. Alternatively, play the audio recording of the extract on Kerboodle: 4.3 Wheelchair users audio.

- Take feedback from the 'Ready, set, go!' task, ensuring students have identified the couple's experiences correctly.

- To test basic comprehension of the extract, ask students to complete the 4.3 Wheelchair users quiz on Kerboodle. This can be completed as a whole-class activity or individually.

**Resources**
◇ Kerboodle: 4.3 Wheelchair users audio
◇ Kerboodle: 4.3 Wheelchair users quiz

## Word power (p110)

- For Activity 3, ensure that students understand that, in the context of the passage, 'confined' means 'limited to'.

- For Activity 4, discuss how the idea of acceptance can be linked to ideas of tolerance and understanding. Ask students to think of a word or phrase that means the opposite (e.g. prejudice, alienation).

- Use the 4.3 Word power worksheet to reinforce students' understanding of vocabulary in the source text, and to extend their ability to use it in a wider context.

**Resources**

◊ Kerboodle: 4.3 Word power worksheet

## Knowledge and understanding (p111)

- After Activities 1 and 2, ask students to consider *why* some people may behave in a different way when confronted with a disabled person. If necessary, give them some sentence starters as prompts, e.g.

  ◊ People treat disability differently because…
  ◊ If they are not used to seeing someone with a disability, people do not…

  If necessary, guide students to consider people's (incorrect) assumptions about physical disability, social awkwardness and embarrassment.

- Before students tackle Activity 5, revise the key skills of summarising. Remind them to look for the key points and to cut out unnecessary words. Limit the summary to 30 words. Students could work in pairs, then share the results with the whole class.

## Writing skills (p112)

- Activity 1 gives students a clear model for letter writing. Display the text or give them copies, so they can highlight and annotate the text to show the structure.

- If necessary, recap with students the differences between the present tense and the past tense before they tackle Activity 2. Use simple examples to begin with, e.g. Today I <u>am</u> team captain (present tense); Yesterday I <u>was</u> team captain (past tense).

- Before students start Activity 3, recap the pronouns: 'I' – first-person singular; 'we' – first person plural; 'you'– second person singular and plural; 'he, she, it' – third person singular; 'they' – third person plural. Some students may find a simple tabulation of this easiest to grasp. When responding to the activity, ensure that students understand that the shift in pronouns to 'we' and 'you' is explicitly designed to promote the feelings of shared involvement and responsibility.

- Use the 4.3 Inclusive language worksheet on Kerboodle to reinforce students' understanding of the effect of inclusive language.

- In Activity 4, challenge students to think of a replacement text for 'are still people', e.g. 'have the same rights', 'are human beings'. Discuss which expression creates the most empathy.

**Resources**

◊ Kerboodle: 4.3 Inclusive language worksheet

## Check your skills (p113)

- The final activity is to construct a letter that makes an emotional plea to shopkeepers to treat people with equal regard and young people with less mistrust.

- Collect ideas about different personal experiences that could be used in the letter.

- If necessary, suggest sentence starters to support ideas:

  ◊ How would you feel if…
  ◊ Would you wish your child to…
  ◊ Children are citizens of this country too…
  ◊ I sympathise with your reasons for doing this, but…

# Unit focus

## Preparation and resources

- Student Book 1: pages 114–119
- Workbook 1: pages 38–39
- Kerboodle resources:
  ◇ 4.4 Playing Out audio
  ◇ 4.4 Playing Out quiz
  ◇ 4.4 Word power worksheet
  ◇ 4.4 Organising information worksheet
- Grammatical knowledge: adverb, conjunction
- Key terms: adverb, conjunction, inference, prefix, suffix (WB), synonym, verb

## What this unit teaches and how

- This unit explores an extract from the Playing Out website, which campaigns for more outside-play areas and facilities for children to play unaccompanied. The activities guide students to focus on how the language, structure and content are designed to influence a particular audience.

- *Catapult Workbook 1* supports and develops the skills in this unit through a factsheet from the Plastic Pollution Coalition. The factsheet focuses on the ways in which the world is being damaged by waste plastics and students explore the persuasive techniques the writer uses.

## Skills and objectives

In this unit, students will:

- Make inferences, using evidence from the text to support their ideas.

- Read closely to analyse how a writer uses language, and selects and contrasts information, to persuade.

- Learn, understand and practise using new vocabulary.

# Teaching suggestions and guidance

This unit is designed to cover two to three lessons, depending on the ability level of your students and the length of lesson time.

### Introduction to the unit (p114)

- Ask students to discuss the games they most enjoyed playing when they were little. Draw out how much or how little they were allowed to play outside unsupervised. If appropriate, share an anecdote about your own outdoor playing as a child. Guide students towards the idea that different generations are encouraged to play in different ways and have access to different leisure options.

### Engaging with the source text (p115)

- Read the text or, alternatively, play the audio recording of the extract on Kerboodle: 4.4 Playing Out audio.

- Take feedback on the 'Ready, set, go!' task. Draw out how the writer is telling the reader of all the advantages of playing out, using a bulleted list and reminding the reader of their own childhood.

- To test basic comprehension of the extract, ask students to complete the 4.4 Playing Out quiz on Kerboodle. This can be completed as a whole-class activity or individually.

**Resources**
◇ Kerboodle: 4.4 Playing Out audio
◇ Kerboodle: 4.4 Playing Out quiz

## Word power (pp116–117)

- For Activity 2, students may need guiding towards an accurate explanation of the meaning of 'unstructured play' in the context. Draw out that it reflects the spontaneity of imaginative play, i.e. not organised by adults with rules and boundaries, but self-regulated.

- If Activity 3 reveals that students need more practice with synonyms, encourage them to think of synonyms for all the given words. If appropriate, guide them to the use of a thesaurus.

- In Activity 4, link the importance of negotiation skills for children to the wider issue of communication skills in later life. Draw attention to the picture and caption. Children who are unable to negotiate may have difficulty in reaching agreements in adult life. Ask students to argue this point by developing the following sentence:

  ◊ It is important to learn to negotiate with others as a child because…

- Use the 4.4 Word power worksheet on Kerboodle to reinforce students' understanding of the target words, and to explore the prefixes 'inter' and 'un'.

**Resources**
◊ Kerboodle: 4.4 Word power worksheet

## Knowledge and understanding (p118)

- Activity 2 asks for a paragraph explaining one reason for there being less outside play nowadays. Students in separate groups could be given different reasons, then asked to present their ideas to the rest of the class. Students can then agree on the most persuasively explained reason.

- For Activity 3, guide students to consider both physical and emotional resilience.

- If students need more support in responding to Activity 5, ask them to think about how emotional outbursts like tantrums in toddlers might be seen in adulthood if people don't learn to control their feelings and responses.

## Reading skills (pp118–119)

- Activities 1 and 2 should build on prior discussion of the subject as well as specific comment on the text.

- If students need more support with Activity 2a, give them a sentence starter, such as:

  ◊ In the past, children regularly played outside unsupervised, whereas…

- If students need more help with Activity 2b, guide them to think about the effect of comparisons, putting two things side by side to evaluate them.

- Use the 4.4 Organising information worksheet on Kerboodle to reinforce students' understanding of bullet points in a text, including support on how to construct effective and accurate bullet point lists.

**Resource**
◊ Kerboodle: 4.4 Organising information worksheet

## Check your skills (p119)

- If students need more support in completing this task, use discussion to recap on ideas. For example, identify some persuasive words and phrases before students start to write, such as: 'for most people', 'adventures', 'happy, well-adjusted adults', 'play freely'.

- If necessary, provide sentence starters to help frame students' responses. For example:

  ◊ The writer lists the reasons that… The effect of this list is to…
  ◊ The writer uses words that build up a picture of…
  ◊ The comparison of past and present experiences shows that…

# Assessment suggestions and guidance

## Why are we assessing this?

Students have completed the chapter on Opinion and persuasion, exploring these aspects through a variety of high-quality non-fiction speeches and texts. The units have reinforced and developed the essential reading and writing skills outlined below, consolidating knowledge and increasing students' confidence.

This assessment unit gives students and teachers the opportunity to assess and reflect on how firmly these skills – in particular, the writing skills – have been grasped and how effectively students can employ them in an assessment situation.

## What are students demonstrating?

Students are asked to demonstrate their ability in using the following features in their persuasive text:

- lists to give examples and emphasis
- repetition to provide rhythm and make memorable patterns
- personal experience
- language chosen to make the reader feel a particular emotion (e.g. anger, empathy)
- pronouns to include the reader (we) and to address the reader (you)
- contrast of images and ideas
- use of past and present tense to urge the need for action
- verbs, adjectives and adverbs chosen for effect
- rhetorical questions for dramatic effect.

## How to deliver the assessment

- Writing extended texts under pressure of time can be challenging for lower-attaining students. The level of support required will vary, depending on students' needs and confidence.
- Ensure that all students are clear about what is required for the task before they start work on it. Discuss the suggested stages of planning, drafting and editing, and recap on the writing techniques they are expected to use.
- Ideally the assessment should be completed in one session but for students who require most support

it may be helpful to split it into stages, with some verbal prompts between stages and the writing of paragraphs. This staged approach will build the confidence of weaker students as they see their skills develop.

- Students could each choose one of the three tasks or all could work on the same task to enable whole-class planning and preparation.
- If students would benefit from sentence starters, you could provide the following options:

### Task A (Letter)

◊ How would you feel if you had nowhere… ?
◊ I have completed a survey involving many young people and…
◊ Having an outdoor space to play is so important because…
◊ The facility would also benefit people of all ages because…

### Task B (Speech)

◊ How many of you remember playing outside…?
◊ You have the power to save the next generation…
◊ The health benefits for the future are guaranteed because…
◊ Do not let down the next generation of children by…

### Task C (Leaflet)

◊ Are you frustrated at having nowhere for your children to… ?
◊ Community spirit will improve because everyone will have the opportunity to…
◊ If we are successful in this bid, children will be able to…
◊ Have no fear – your children will be safe and secure because…

## How to mark the assessment

You will want to mark this in line with departmental and school marking guidelines. If you wish, you could use the *Catapult* marking scales (provided on Kerboodle). The *Catapult* marking scales are designed to assess lower attaining students who need to consolidate skills which have not yet been fully grasped but need to be secured and developed in order to move those students forward and narrow the gap between their existing levels of achievement and national expectations for KS3.

Using the *Catapult* marking scales will help you to identify specific strengths and areas for improvement in an individual student's reading. This may help you to set development targets as well as building a profile of your class as writers.

## Following up the assessment

The assessment should enable you to identify clear areas in which students have underperformed and you can therefore plan in detail how to reinforce understanding using *Catapult* resources.

1. Refer to the *Catapult* mapping grids on pages 132-135 of this Teacher Book to identify other *Catapult* chapters where these reading and writing skills are covered. For example:

   ◇ language chosen to make the reader feel a particular emotion (e.g. anger, empathy) is also covered in Chapter 6 (Unit 4)

   ◇ contrasting images and ideas is also covered in Chapter 6 (Unit 3)

   ◇ verbs, adjectives and adverbs chosen for effect are also covered in Chapter 1 (Unit 1) and Chapter 6 (Unit 2).

2. Direct students to the SPaG quizzes on Kerboodle to address any areas of weakness that the assessment may have revealed. For example, basic skills can be reinforced with the following quizzes:

   ◇ Capital letters
   ◇ Full stops
   ◇ Commas
   ◇ Sentences
   ◇ Pronouns
   ◇ Adverbs.

   Encourage students to proofread their work, looking for ways of making their writing style more concise and fluent. For example, skills can be reinforced with the following quizzes:

   ◇ Noun phrases
   ◇ Adverbials
   ◇ Conjunctions
   ◇ Parenthesis
   ◇ Verbs and tenses.

The Grammar reference guide on Kerboodle contains definitions and additional examples of each of the spelling, punctuation and grammar points covered in the quizzes, for your reference.

3. If students' vocabulary seems limited, remind them to make use of the target words they have explored, which are also contained in the target word list at the back of the Student Book. Students may also benefit from compiling their own vocabulary lists for reference. These should be shared and discussed regularly.

### Resources
◇ Kerboodle: *Catapult* marking scales
◇ Kerboodle: SPaG quizzes
◇ Kerboodle: Grammar reference guide

Note that the source texts and activities in *Catapult Workbook 1* can also be used as assessment material, if students haven't already used them to consolidate their learning from the Student Book.

# Chapter 5: Experience and advice

## Chapter overview

### Why are we teaching this?

Understanding how writers recount their experiences and offer advice effectively is an important part of appreciating many forms of non-fiction texts. By exploring high-quality extracts, selected to be accessible and appealing, students can then develop their own writing in the same forms through carefully supported activities.

Across the four units and in the final assessment in this chapter, students will read a wide variety of non-fiction. The texts range from a late 19th-century guide for wealthy women travellers, to the contemporary account of an exhilarating parachute jump from a website devoted to skydiving. Students are given an opportunity to use the analytical skills they have practised in the reading assessment at the end of the chapter.

Many activities in this chapter will benefit from discussion prior to students completing a written response. Encourage students to elaborate and explain clearly their understanding and ideas. Speaking and listening skills are an important prerequisite to developing effective reading and writing skills, so they should be an integral part of each unit.

### What are the learning aims?

In every unit in this chapter, students will learn to strengthen the core skills of:

- learning, understanding and practising using new vocabulary
- increasing general knowledge and contextual understanding.

In addition, each unit will focus on the following learning aims. Students will:

| Unit 1 | Unit 2 | Unit 3 | Unit 4 |
|---|---|---|---|
| • Explore how verb tense and structure can be used effectively to describe an experience.<br>• Use these features to make their own writing more effective.<br>• Learn, understand and practise using new vocabulary. | • Make inferences and predictions using evidence from the text.<br>• Explore figurative language choices made by the writer.<br>• Learn, understand and practise using new vocabulary. | • Find key details from a text and present them in a different context to demonstrate understanding.<br>• Explore how a writer uses sentence structure and paragraph structure and punctuation to build tension.<br>• Learn, understand and practise using new vocabulary. | • Identify information from a 19th-century text and work out implied meanings.<br>• Explore how language features are used to communicate advice.<br>• Learn, understand and practise using new vocabulary. |

### How will this chapter be assessed?

The reading assessment at the end of the chapter uses an extract from *I Am, I Am, I Am: Seventeen Brushes with Death* by Maggie O'Farrell to help students practise the reading analysis skills developed throughout the chapter.

The focus for assessment will be:

- analysing language techniques, such as choice of vocabulary and sentence structure
- exploring how tension is created through verb tenses, word choice and punctuation.

Note that the short 'Check your skills' feature at the end of every unit in this chapter provides formative assessment opportunities to support students' learning.

## Chapter 5 unit sequence

The sequence of units is designed so that students gain in confidence as they complete more challenging activities while progressing through the chapter.

Note that some activities feature in just the Teacher Book (TB).

| | Chapter 5: Experience and advice | |
|---|---|---|
| | **Student Book** | **Workbook** |
| **1: Adrenaline rush** | **Source text:** Blog post about skydiving from the website 'Adventure Living'<br><br>• Discuss vicarious emotions and/or experiences students have felt from reading or watching films. (TB)<br>• Analyse the use of words that describe the visceral effect of skydiving and how the reader is led to share this.<br>• Analyse how the writer uses the passage of time to effectively convey the speed of the fall from the aircraft.<br>• Use the same skills to write the imagined account of an astronaut on board a rocket being launched into space. | **Source text:** *More Than This* by Patrick Ness<br><br>• Revise verb tenses.<br>• Write in the present tense to add a sense of immediacy for the reader. |
| **2: When the soldiers came** | **Source text:** *Bitter Herbs* by Marga Minco<br><br>• Discuss the subject of the Holocaust and remind students that, in the Second World War, millions of people were taken by soldiers to concentration camps and detention centres. (TB)<br>• Analyse the use of language in the extract that describes the effect of the soldiers and Marga's strong character.<br>• Create some imagined dialogue between a soldier and an officer. Perform the scenes.<br>• Explain how the reader can infer aspects of Marga's character from evidence in the text. | **Source text:** *I am Malala* by Malala Yousafzai<br><br>• Explore the use of inference.<br>• Analyse figurative language. |
| **3: Confrontation** | **Source text:** 'The day I survived a very grizzly bear attack' by Guy Grieve<br><br>• Discuss a time when students felt that their life, or the life of a friend or family member, was in danger. (TB)<br>• Write a short account using the target words from the text.<br>• Analyse the writer's use of language and the way tension is created.<br>• Write a text describing an encounter with an escaped cheetah from the local zoo. | **Source text:** *The Serengeti Rules* by Sean B. Carroll<br><br>• Explore writing techniques used to create tension, including questions, dashes and adverbs.<br>• Rewrite an account, adding punctuation and changing the wording and sentence structures to heighten the tension. |
| **4: Advice for Victorian women** | **Source text:** *Hints to Lady Travellers* by Lillias Campbell Davidson<br><br>• Discuss when women were allowed to vote. Develop this into a discussion about the limitations on Victorian women's lives. (TB)<br>• Practise using the target words from the text in a new context.<br>• Analyse the grammar in multi-clause sentences and rewrite them in a simpler style.<br>• Comment on the validity of the advice in today's context. | **Source text:** *Advice to a Mother* by Pye Henry Chavasse<br><br>• Identify information from a 19th-century text.<br>• Explore how language features are used to convey advice, in particular emotive vocabulary and rhetorical questions. |

| Chapter 5: Experience and advice | |
|---|---|
| **Student Book** | **Workbook** |

<table>
<tr>
<td rowspan="2">Reading assessment</td>
<td>

**Source text:** Extract 1 and Extract 2 from *I Am, I Am, I Am: Seventeen Brushes with Death* by Maggie O'Farrell

- Identify 'true or false' details from the text.
- Explain what makes language effective in the description of thoughts and feelings.
- Explain how the writer creates tension, with given criteria for language and text structure.

</td>
<td></td>
</tr>
</table>

# Preparing to teach

## Refresh your knowledge

You might find it helpful to refer to the following key points when planning the teaching of this chapter:

- All the non-fiction extracts in this chapter are linked to danger, either in the form of dramatic accounts of extreme experiences or of giving advice to prepare for dangerous encounters. All the writers of these texts are aiming to convey a sense of tension and drama to their readers, and they use specific technical features in the language, structure and presentation of their texts to do this effectively.

- Recounts of dramatic experiences can be found in numerous non-fiction genres, including autobiographies, travel books, newspaper and magazine articles, websites and blogs. The popularity of such texts endures because they expand the reader's experience beyond the life they know but are still rooted in reality, unlike fiction. They provide the opportunity to experience different places and situations vicariously, offering the thrill of danger and drama without any actual threat to the reader personally.

- Historically, travel writers have not only recounted their experiences, but also issued advice for those considering similar journeys. One of the first 'travel guides' was written in the 12th century for pilgrims heading to Santiago de Compostela in Spain. A monk, Aymeric Picaud, recorded the route, terrain and rivers that pilgrims would encounter, plus some (rather prejudiced) description of the local inhabitants. This guide is known as the *Codex Calixtinus*, as it is prefaced with a letter to Pope Calixtus II.

- Travel writing was particularly popular in the Renaissance and then again in the 19th century, when the railways made travel more accessible to more people than ever before. Nowadays, travel blogs are particularly popular, as travellers can relay their experiences almost instantaneously to their readers.

- Diaries and memoirs have the advantage of being written to reflect on personal experiences with the benefit of distance, as opposed to the more immediate eye-witness type of account, such as those found in travel blogs and the bear-attack extract by Guy Grieve. Students should be aware of the perspectives that different forms of writing encourage.

## Links and further reading

- There is a focus on personal experience in the source texts for three of the units. More extracts can be accessed from a range of websites that describe memorable and dramatic events, e.g. *The Guardian* website at: https://www.theguardian.com/lifeandstyle/2017/dec/29/experience-i-was-crushed-by-a-log. Note that the content of these can sometimes be adult and challenging, so you should explore them fully before directing students towards them.

- For more about the history of skydiving, see the British Parachuting Association website: http://www.bpa.org.uk/about-us/history-of-the-sport/. There have been some amazing formation jumps made – find out more and perhaps use some examples such as the world record formation jump with students at: https://www.youtube.com/watch?v=CogIXrea6A4.
- Students may be interested to read the detailed factfile explaining the planning and execution of the absolute world record for any free-fall set by Felix Baumgartner in 2012. See http://www.redbullstratos.com/the-mission/world-record-jump/.
- Students can read other advice texts about escaping from wild animals and explore how the information is presented in websites such as: https://nypost.com/2017/05/12/how-to-escape-from-any-wild-animal/. The *New York Post* article begins by commenting on what to do about bears.
- A large number of books published in the Victorian era were designed to help parents prepare their daughters for the life expected of them as wives and mothers. Many examples can be found at the British Library: https://www.bl.uk/collection-items/conduct-book-for-women#.

## Planning guidance and teaching tips

Think about how you can make the materials relevant to your students and responsive to their particular needs and learning targets. Some suggested approaches to address key areas are provided below.

- Encourage discussion of students' wider reading wherever possible, particularly in relation to recounts of dramatic experiences or travel advice. Any source of reading should be valued and encouraged, e.g. from magazines and the Internet. Many lower-attaining students won't have built up much reading stamina or have the confidence or inclination to read much independently.
- Continue to praise students as often as possible so that their improvement in skills is not just seen through higher scores in assessments. Choose a particular form of writing linked to the units studied in this chapter and organise a competition, e.g. for the best narrative dealing with a life-or-death experience.
- All the target words are in the target word list at the back of the Student Book. Encourage students to use this to establish the habit of looking up words as part of the process of discussing and exploring their meaning.
- Use strategies to maintain students' engagement in the texts and activities, such as setting limited times for responses, making some activities more competitive or conducting quick quizzes to check comprehension.
- Refer to the Grammar reference guide on Kerboodle for definitions and exemplars of specific grammar and punctuation terms covered in this chapter. Kerboodle also provides quizzes to help improve the technical accuracy of students' writing and the application of grammar in context.

# Unit focus

## Preparation and resources

- Student Book 1: pages 122–127
- Workbook 1: pages 40–41
- Kerboodle resources:
  ◇ 5.1 Adventure Living audio
  ◇ 5.1 Adventure Living quiz
  ◇ 5.1 Word power worksheet
  ◇ 5.1 Past and present tense worksheet
- Grammatical knowledge: past tense, present tense
- Key terms: metaphor, narrate (WB), past tense, phrase (WB), prefix, present tense, setting (WB), structure, synonym, verb, verb tenses

## What this unit teaches and how

- The extract from a skydiving website is used to demonstrate an effective recount of the experience of skydiving (with the aid of a parachute). Activities support students in exploring how the writer structures the passage, using metaphor and verb tenses to convey the thrill of the experience to the reader. Students then use the same features to write their own account of a being inside a rocket when it is launched.

- *Catapult Workbook 1* supports and further develops the skills in this unit through a short extract from the novel, *More Than This* by Patrick Ness. The extract describes someone being attacked and uses the present tense to intensify the experience for the reader.

## Skills and objectives

In this unit, students will:

- Explore how verb tense and structure can be used effectively to describe an experience.

- Use these features to make their own writing more effective.

- Learn, understand and practise using new vocabulary.

# Teaching suggestions and guidance

This unit is designed to cover two to three lessons, depending on the ability level of your students and the length of lesson time.

## Introduction to the unit (p122)

- Ask students to discuss whether they think that reading about an experience or watching it on film can ever be a substitute for actual personal experience. The discussion could cover fiction, non-fiction and film. The consensus should be that it is entirely dependent on the experience being described and the quality of the depiction.

- Widen discussion to encompass the future role of virtual reality in human experience, not just in computer games but also in training people for vital roles such as doctors and pilots.

## Engaging with the source text (p123)

- Play a film of a sky dive on the IWB, e.g. an extract from https://www.youtube.com/watch?v=8ojRSqHPQXM. Turn off either the sound or the visuals, and ask students to think of words that seem to best describe the visual or aural experience.

- Read the source text aloud or, alternatively, play the audio recording of the extract on Kerboodle: 5.1 Adventure Living audio.

- Take feedback on students' thoughts about the 'Ready, set, go!' task. Discuss what feelings students predict for themselves and compare them to what the writer describes.

- To test basic comprehension of the extract, ask students to complete the 5.1 Adventure Living quiz on Kerboodle. This can be completed as a whole-class activity or individually.

**Resources**
◇ Kerboodle: 5.1 Adventure Living audio
◇ Kerboodle: 5.1 Adventure Living quiz

## Word power (pp124–125)

- For Activity 1, students may need prompts to suggest experiences. Guide them towards activities such as riding a rollercoaster, skateboarding, sliding on ice. Ask for some alternative words for 'exhilarating', e.g. thrilling, incomparable, breathtaking.

- For Activity 2, introduce the word 'intensifies' and ask students to explain why it can be used in a similar way to 'heightens'.

- For Activity 3, ask students to find an alternative word that can be used in place of 'scant', e.g. mere.

- The explanation of the metaphorical use of 'in tune' in Activity 5 can be compared to the phrase 'at one' (as in: at one with nature), which has a similar sentiment. If students need support, suggest 'calm', 'peaceful', 'serene' as descriptions of the skydiver's feelings.

- For Activity 6, as well as reminding students to use some of the target vocabulary, suggest they try to include some imagery, using metaphor, e.g.

  ◇ pushing the boundaries…
  ◇ stretching possibility…
  ◇ bursting with energy…

- Use the 5.1 Word power worksheet on Kerboodle to reinforce and develop students' confidence with the target words, and the use of the prefix 're'.

**Resources**
◇ Kerboodle: 5.1 Word power worksheet

## Knowledge and understanding (p126)

- The activities in this section could be completed in pairs, or in a quiz format, with all questions being answered first, then responses shared as a class.

- Draw attention to the image and the question in the caption. Do students think they would enjoy doing a similar jump and want to repeat it? Encourage them to explain their responses, referring to information in the source text.

- Focus students on the word 'victorious' if they need guidance in responding to the question in Activity 4.

## Writing skills (pp126–127)

- Use the 5.1 Past and present tense worksheet on Kerboodle to reinforce students' understanding of these concepts, before they tackle Activity 1.

- For Activity 2, if necessary, remind students of the meaning of 'structure/structured'. It may help them to think about the physical shape of the text in terms of paragraphs.

- If students struggle with Activity 4, support them by suggesting that the references are used to exaggerate for emphasis, e.g. 'slows time' and 'eternity'.

**Resources**
◇ Kerboodle: 5.1 Past and present tense worksheet

## Check your skills (p127)

- Some students could tackle this writing task independently, but others may benefit from some prior discussion and guidance on vocabulary and ideas.

- Discuss and list some adjectives that could be used to describe the feelings of the astronaut, e.g. tense, prepared, thoughtful, etc.

- Support students with some sentence starters that can be used for each of the listed techniques:

  ◇ At last I can carry out my training for real…
  ◇ It is too late to turn back but I feel…
  ◇ The clock seems to have slowed down…
  ◇ I look at the photo of my family and realise I have paid them scant attention during the long weeks of training.

# Unit focus

## Preparation and resources

- Student Book 1: pages 128–133
- Workbook 1: pages 42–43
- Kerboodle resources:
  ◊ 5.2 Bitter Herbs audio
  ◊ 5.2 Bitter Herbs quiz
  ◊ 5.2 Word power worksheet
  ◊ 5.2 Figurative language worksheet
- Grammatical knowledge: noun, phrase
- Key terms: autobiography (WB), chronicle, dialogue, figurative language, infer, inference, noun, phrase, simile

## What this unit teaches and how

- The extract from *Bitter Herbs* by Marga Minco describes a frightening episode where a young girl is nearly picked up for transportation to a concentration camp in 1940s Amsterdam. The activities focus students on what is inferred through the text and the effect of the figurative language in the extract.

- *Catapult Workbook 1* supports and develops the skills in this unit through analysing an extract from *I am Malala* by Malala Yousafzai. Students are asked to explore the way that language is used to reflect the dramatic details of an attack when Malala was shot by extremists and left for dead.

## Skills and objectives

In this unit, students will:

- Make inferences and predictions using evidence from the text

- Explore figurative language choices made by the writer.

- Learn, understand and practise using new vocabulary.

# Teaching suggestions and guidance

This unit is designed to cover two to three lessons, depending on the ability level of your students and the length of lesson time.

### Introduction to the unit (p128)

- Discuss what students know about the Holocaust. Ask them in groups to arrive at five key points that everyone should know about the subject. Gather feedback and ensure that there are no misunderstandings. Fill in any gaps in their knowledge that would prevent them from understanding the context of the source text.

- Ask students to suggest words that link to the terrible ways people are treated in all wars, e.g. tragedy, helpless, persecuted, cruelty, oppressed. Ask students to keep the lists and add to them as they progress through the unit.

### Engaging with the source text (p129)

- Choose an appropriate image to show civilians being treated in an aggressive way by soldiers of occupation, e.g. https://twitter.com/doamuslims/status/751853287645843456. The aim is to show that civilians are almost always powerless. However, when using such images, be aware of any sensitivities that might be particular to your students.

- Read the extract aloud or, alternatively, play the audio recording of the extract on Kerboodle: 5.2 Bitter Herbs audio.

- Take feedback from students about their response to the 'Ready, set, go!' task. Draw out observations about the bravery and strong personality of Marga in standing up for herself when confronted by the soldiers.

- To test basic comprehension of the extract, ask students to complete the 5.2 Bitter Herbs quiz on Kerboodle. This can be completed as a whole-class activity or individually.

**Resources**
◊ Kerboodle: 5.2 Bitter Herbs audio
◊ Kerboodle: 5.2 Bitter Herbs quiz

## Word power (p130)

- For Activity 1, guide students towards the negative connotations of the word 'immobile'. Ask what this word suggests about the soldiers. (They are robotic, unfeeling, unemotional, uncaring.)

- In Activity 2, ask students to think of adverbs with a similar meaning to 'decidedly'. Guide them towards words such as: strongly, determinedly, stubbornly, resolutely.

- In addition to finding 'banged' and 'heavy' (footsteps) for Activity 4, support students with thinking about the effect of these words on the reader. For example, the sounds are linked directly to the threat of an invading force, oppression and something that cannot be stopped.

- Use the 5.2 Word power worksheet to reinforce students' understanding of the vocabulary used in the source text, through the use of synonyms.

**Resources**
◊ Kerboodle: 5.2 Word power worksheet

## Knowledge and understanding (p131)

- In Activity 4, support pairs of students in creating two versions of dramatic scenes using the imagined dialogue between the soldier and the officer. Set criteria such as four sentences from each character in each scene. If students need more guidance, suggest that the soldier is annoyed with Marga but the officer is sticking to the orders that he has been given.

- Share performances of some dialogues with the whole class. Encourage constructive feedback from observing students, commenting on the choice of language and effectiveness of the performance.

- Set a time for students to write their answers to the questions in Activity 5. Then ask them to swap with a partner to have their answers assessed. Go through the responses together.

## Reading skills (p132-133)

- Ensure that students link their choices of words in Activity 1 to a piece of evidence from the text. If they require more support, offer the following sentence starters:

  ◊ We know that she is desperate because…
  ◊ The writer shows that Marga is quick-witted by the way she…

- For Activity 3, students need to write Marga's thoughts in the first person to describe the way she is feeling. Support students with some advice for structuring sentences, such as:

  ◊ My blood runs cold at the sight of the face that will decide…
  ◊ I feel my life depends on what I say next…
  ◊ What if the officer agrees with the soldier? Am I doomed to disappear to… ?

- Use the 5.2 Figurative language worksheet on Kerboodle to reinforce and develop students' understanding of this concept using examples from the source text.

**Resources**
◊ Kerboodle: 5.2 Figurative language worksheet

## Check your skills (p133)

- Support students in explaining the effect of the highlighted text on readers. Guide them to consider the image of a scrap of paper being trodden on. What image of power and vulnerability does this suggest? What does the description of 'green steel' suggest about the soldier's head/mind? (Draw students towards the strong, powerful, unyielding nature of steel.)

- In Activity 2, remind students to use verbs to describe what a writer has 'done' to help the reader to infer aspects of her character, e.g. *explains, describes, portrays, illustrates*.

- Students could swap their first draft with a partner and proofread for errors in spelling, punctuation and grammar. Students then swap back and write a final draft.

# Unit focus

## Preparation and resources

- Student Book 1: pages 134–139
- Workbook 1: pages 44–45
- Kerboodle resources:
  - ◊ 5.3 The day I survived a very grizzly bear attack audio
  - ◊ 5.3 The day I survived a very grizzly bear attack quiz
  - ◊ 5.3 Word power worksheet
  - ◊ 5.3 Guiding a reader through a text worksheet
- Grammatical knowledge: adverb, dash
- Key terms: adverb, context, dash, sentence structure

## What this unit teaches and how

- The extract from 'The day I survived a very grizzly bear attack' by Guy Grieve describes a terrifying confrontation with a black bear. The activities in this unit focus students on identifying key information in the source text and exploring how tension is built up.

- *Catapult Workbook 1* supports and develops the skills in this unit through an extract from *The Serengeti Rules* by Sean B. Carroll. The text describes a close encounter with elephants while camping.

## Skills and objectives

In this unit, students will:

- Find key details from a text and present them in a different context to demonstrate understanding.

- Explore how a writer uses sentence structure and paragraph structure and punctuation to build tension.

- Learn, understand and practise using new vocabulary.

# Teaching suggestions and guidance

This unit is designed to cover two to three lessons, depending on the ability level of your students and the length of lesson time.

## Introduction to the unit (p134)

- Ask students to discuss a time when they have felt that their life, or the life of a friend or family member, was in danger. Gather feedback, focusing in particular on how students describe their thoughts and feelings at that time. Explain the subject of the extract.

- Encourage students to gather vocabulary linked to life-threatening situations as they work through this unit.

## Engaging with the source text (p135)

- Display the extract and read it aloud. Ask students to highlight/underline words that relate to the bear's behaviour and characteristics in one colour and the references to the narrator's actions and feelings in another. Students will discover that the majority of the text involves the description of the bear.

- Alternatively, play the audio recording of the extract on Kerboodle: 5.3 The day I survived a very grizzly bear attack audio.

- Take feedback on the 'Ready, set, go!' task. Ensure students can back up their ideas with close reference to the text.

- To test basic comprehension of the extract, ask students to complete the 5.3 The day I survived a very grizzly bear attack quiz on Kerboodle. This can be completed as a whole-class activity or individually.

### Resources
- ◊ Kerboodle: 5.3 The day I survived a very grizzly bear attack audio
- ◊ Kerboodle: 5.3 The day I survived a very grizzly bear attack quiz

## Word power (pp136–137)

- For Activity 1, ask students to explain why the word 'agility' may be surprising. Link this to the static image of a bear and the well-known act of hibernation, which links to the idea of sleep and laziness.

- Gather students' responses to Activity 3. Discuss the range of responses and note the following if they are not included: he feels safe; he thinks he has escaped death; he thinks the bear has avoided the confrontation.

- Support students with Activity 4 by suggesting the following sentence starters:

  ◇ Feeling worried that I would be caught…
  ◇ Hoping that my arrival had been unseen…

  Note that students can write in the first or third person, i.e. from the point of view of themselves or a character of their own invention.

- Use the 5.3 Word power worksheet to reinforce and develop students' confidence in using the target words in this unit.

### Resources
◇ Kerboodle: 5.3 Word power worksheet

## Knowledge and understanding (p137)

- For Activity 3, suggest that students note down references to the bear under two headings: 'Physical characteristics' and 'Behaviour'. These notes can then be worked into full sentences using quotations from the text.

- Model how to start a chart of Dos and Don'ts on the IWB, e.g. a Do (show them respect) and a Don't (underestimate). Students can add to this creatively, but ultimately strip the ideas down to the key principles for the final agreed lists.

- Use the 5.3 Guiding a reader through a text worksheet on Kerboodle to reinforce students' understanding of how adverbs and dashes can be used to guide a reader through a text.

### Resources
◇ Kerboodle: 5.3 Guiding a reader through a text worksheet

## Writing skills (pp138–139)

- Support students' understanding of the use of the three given adverbs (suddenly, then, now) and how to structure the paragraph. If necessary, give another example, such as: **Suddenly**, the noise level of the plane engines increased to a deafening level and I had to cover my ears. **Then** I tried to turn away from the wind and the dust. **Now** I wished I had paid more attention during my training!

- For Activity 2, which asks students to explain what difference the inclusion of a dash in the text makes to the overall impact on the reader, suggest a sentence starter such as:

  ◇ The dash alters the impact of the sentence because…

- Activity 3 looks at the way the focus moves back and forth from the bear to Grieve. The annotations could be completed together on the IWB. Alternatively, create sentences with similar structures and complete the analysis on the IWB before students deal with the sentences in the extract.

## Check your skills (p139)

- Students are asked to write a creative narrative about an encounter with an escaped cheetah from the local zoo. As well as the criteria offered, support them with ideas such as:

  ◇ Adverbs such as: momentarily, afterwards, later
  ◇ I saw – or thought I saw – a shape…
  ◇ I could hear its breathing nearby, the noise of my heartbeat…
  ◇ I knew that *assuming* the cheetah didn't see me…

- Encourage students to proofread the first draft of their work for spelling, punctuation and grammatical errors (or proofread their partner's work), then write a final draft including all corrections.

# Unit focus

## Preparation and resources

- Student Book 1: pages 140–145
- Workbook 1: pages 46–47
- Kerboodle resources:
  - ◇ 5.4 Hints to Lady Travellers audio
  - ◇ 5.4 Hints to Lady Travellers quiz
  - ◇ 5.4 Word power worksheet
  - ◇ 5.4 19th-century multi-clause sentences worksheet
- Grammatical knowledge: clause, multi-clause sentence, noun phrase
- Key terms: antonym (WB), clause, emotive language (WB), multi-clause sentence, noun phrase, rhetorical question (WB)

## What this unit teaches and how

- This unit guides students in exploring a 19th-century text, identifying information, working out implied meaning and considering language features. The source text is from *Hints to Lady Travellers* by Lillias Campbell Davidson and is a powerful piece of writing, which reflects the Victorian attitude to women from a female perspective. The writer accepts male primacy at the same time as encouraging women to quell their anxieties in order to be able to travel without the company of men.

- *Catapult Workbook 1* also supports and develops the skills in this unit through an extract from *Advice to a Mother* (1878) by Pye Henry Chavasse. Students are asked to analyse features of the language in the extract and use them in a reply to the points made in the text.

## Skills and objectives

In this unit, students will:

- Identify information from a 19th-century text and work out implied meanings.

- Explore how language features are used to communicate advice.

- Learn, understand and practise using new vocabulary.

# Teaching suggestions and guidance

This unit is designed to cover two to three lessons, depending on the ability level of your students and the length of lesson time.

## Introduction to the unit (p140)

- Ask students why they think women were not allowed to vote in elections until 1918. (Note that even in 1918, women had to be aged over 30 to vote. In 1928, the voting age for women was reduced to 21.) Draw out that women were regarded as less able than men, both physically and mentally.

- Following on from the above, discuss what roles were available to women in Victorian times, e.g. governess, nurse, maidservant, cook, nanny, teacher. Point out that the vast majority of poorer women would have worked in agriculture or factories, usually in dangerous conditions and often with children. Ensure students understand that higher-class women were not expected to work once they were married.

## Engaging with the source text (p141)

- This text may be challenging for some students. Plan the reading carefully so that the unfamiliar words can be understood in the context of the extract. Some students may need words explaining in addition to the glossary words.

- Take feedback from the 'Ready, set, go!' task. Students could work in pairs to come up with three main points to summarise the advice. Guide students towards points such as: be prepared; have a positive outlook; don't fill your mind with anxieties/worry.

- In addition to reading the extract, play the audio recording of the extract on Kerboodle: 5.4 Hints to Lady Travellers audio. Students will benefit from hearing the extract repeated.

- To test basic comprehension of the extract, ask students to complete the 5.4 Hints to Lady Travellers quiz on Kerboodle. This can be completed as a whole-class activity or individually.

**Resources**

◊ Kerboodle: 5.4 Hints to Lady Travellers audio
◊ Kerboodle: 5.4 Hints to Lady Travellers quiz

## Word power (pp142-143)

- Activity 3 should lead students to pinpointing some of the principles that underpin friendship. Take feedback from students' paragraphs and list the main principles on the IWB. Encourage students to express these principles in one word, e.g. loyalty, listening, empathy.

- For Activity 4, guide students in linking this point back to their original discussion about how women were regarded in Victorian times. The key point is that the writer is being practical (because men will instinctively 'protect'). However, the initial effect is to assume that the writer is explaining that women are 'weak' (though she only means physically).

- Use the 5.4 Word power worksheet on Kerboodle to reinforce and develop students' vocabulary linked to the source text in this unit.

**Resources**

◊ Kerboodle: 5.4 Word power worksheet

## Knowledge and understanding (p143)

- Use the 5.4 19th-century multi-clause sentences worksheet on Kerboodle to reinforce students' understanding of how they can break down multi-clause sentences.

- Discuss what is meant by 'a universal rule', in paragraph 3. Ask students whether they think this rule applies to all men, all women or all people.

- Link Activity 5 to the summaries of the main points of advice that students came up with earlier, e.g. the importance of low anxiety and staying calm. Although the writer wants the reader to be prepared, she warns against an over-anxious attitude, which would take all the pleasure out of travelling.

**Resources**

◊ Kerboodle: 5.4 19th-century multi-clause sentences worksheet

## Reading skills (p144-145)

- Activity 1 draws attention to the lexical density of the extract, typical of many 19th-century texts. The grammatical analysis should give students a strategy for working out the meaning of similar texts, by identifying and 'translating' each clause into a simpler, modern version.

- Students may benefit from working in pairs on Activity 1b.

## Check your skills (p145)

- Set a limit of 70 words for the answer to Activity 1 and ask students to work in pairs. They should look at all their answers so far and the ideas discussed at the beginning of the lesson to support their thinking.

- For Activity 3, students will need support to organise their thoughts carefully before writing their paragraph. Creating a plan with an agree/disagree table may be useful.

- Suggest that the writing should deal with no more than three points for each side of the argument. Supportive sentence starters could be given, such as:

  ◊ Although the writer states…
  ◊ I agree with what she explains about… but…
  ◊ She tries to… by…

# Assessment suggestions and guidance

## Why are we assessing this?

Students have completed the chapter on Experience and advice, exploring texts linked to these concepts through a variety of high-quality contemporary, 20th- and 19th-century extracts. The units have reinforced and developed the essential reading and writing skills outlined below, consolidating knowledge and increasing students' confidence.

This assessment unit gives students and teachers the opportunity to assess and reflect on how firmly these skills – in particular, the reading skills – have been grasped and how effectively students can employ them in an assessment situation.

## What are students demonstrating?

Students are asked to:

- identify information implied within the extracts
- make inferences and predictions using evidence from the text
- explore figurative language choices made by the writer
- explore how a writer uses verb tense, word choice, sentence structure and punctuation to create tension
- evaluate the extracts against a given viewpoint, supporting their assertions with evidence from the text.

## How to deliver the assessment

- The reading assessment is based on an extract from the text *I Am, I Am, I Am: Seventeen Brushes with Death* by Maggie O'Farrell. Written in the first person, this is an accessible text for most readers but you may wish to read the text aloud during the assessment, even re-reading extracts linked to particular questions to further support students. Audio recordings of the extracts are available on Kerboodle: 5.5 I Am, I Am, I Am extract 1 audio and 5.5 I Am, I Am, I Am extract 2 audio.
- For students who still find the development of text analysis challenging, the assessment unit could be broken down into individual activities. Success in shorter activities will help to instil the confidence

needed to achieve or move closer to learning targets.

- Where appropriate, students may be supported by allowing time to discuss what is expected in the assessment activities. This could be done for the assessment as a whole or on a question-by-question basis.
- For more confident students, the assessment can be used in its entirety, to be completed under exam-type conditions within a set time limit.
- As this reading assessment asks students to comment on specific grammatical features of the text, you should consider which aspects need revision (e.g. verb tenses and sentence structure) and practise these with students, perhaps leaving explanatory notes and/or presentations in view during the assessment.
- For Question 2, support could guide students towards ideas such as the repetition of 'He can't swim' to emphasise (or exaggerate) the danger.
- For Question 3, support could guide students towards ideas such as the predominance of the present tense, with the past tense used to reflect on a mistake; the range of negative descriptions of the sea; and her failing energy – as well as the lists and direct questions forming the structure of much of the text.

## How to mark the assessment

You will want to mark this in line with departmental and school marking guidelines. If you wish, you could use the *Catapult* marking scales (provided on Kerboodle). The *Catapult* marking scales are designed to assess lower-attaining students who need to consolidate skills that have not yet been fully grasped but need to be secured and developed in order to move those students forward and narrow the gap between their existing levels of achievement and national expectations for KS3.

Using the *Catapult* marking scales will help you to identify specific strengths and areas for improvement in an individual student's reading. This may help you to set development targets as well as build a profile of your class as readers.

## Following up the assessment

The assessment should enable you to identify clear areas in which students have underperformed and you can therefore plan in detail how to reinforce understanding using *Catapult* resources.

1. Refer to the *Catapult* mapping grids on pages 132-135 of this Teacher Book to identify other *Catapult* chapters where these reading and writing skills are covered. For example:

   ◊ identifying implied meaning in the text is also covered in Chapter 2 (Unit 5) and Chapter 3 (Unit 3)

   ◊ identifying key details from the text is also covered in Chapter 1 (Units 1 and 4) and Chapter 2 (Unit 5)

   ◊ focusing on making inferences and prediction is also covered in Chapter 1 (Units 2 and 4), Chapter 4 (Unit 4) and Chapter 6 (Unit 3)

   ◊ focusing on the use of figurative language is also covered in Chapter 1 (Units 1, 2, 3 and 5), Chapter 2 (Units 1, 2, 3, 4 and 5), Chapter 3 (Units 1, 2, 3 and 4), Chapter 4 (Units 1, 2, 3 and 4), Chapter 5 (Units 1, 2, 3 and 5) and Chapter 6 (Units 1, 2, 3 and 4)

   ◊ focusing on the creation of tension through verb tense, word choice, sentence structure, and punctuation is also covered in Chapter 2 (Units 1 and 4)

   ◊ using evidence from the text to support analysis is also covered in Chapter 1 (Units 2, 3, 4 and 5), Chapter 2 (Unit 5) and Chapter 4 (Unit 4).

2. Direct students to the SPaG quizzes on Kerboodle to address any areas of weakness that the assessment may have revealed. For example, basic skills can be reinforced with the following quizzes:

   ◊ Inverted commas
   ◊ Dashes
   ◊ Commas
   ◊ Common and proper nouns
   ◊ Sentences
   ◊ Verbs and tenses.

Encourage students to proofread their work, looking for ways of making their writing style more concise and fluent. For example, skills can be reinforced with the following quizzes:

   ◊ Noun phrases
   ◊ Adverbials
   ◊ Adjectives
   ◊ Adverbs

   ◊ Conjunctions
   ◊ Parenthesis
   ◊ Apostrophes.

The Grammar reference guide on Kerboodle contains definitions and additional examples of each of the spelling, punctuation and grammar points covered in the quizzes, for your reference.

3. If students' vocabulary seems limited, remind them to make use of the target words they have explored, which are also contained in the target word list at the back of the Student Book. Students may also benefit from compiling their own vocabulary lists for reference. These should be shared and discussed regularly.

4. Work with students to increase their confidence in spelling key grammatical and literary terms, e.g. preposition, conjunction, quotation, synonym, adverbial, sentence, exclamation, simile, metaphor, personification. Lower-attaining students may resist using these terms in their writing if they are unsure of spellings, even if they understand the meaning.

### Resources
   ◊ Kerboodle: *Catapult* marking scales
   ◊ Kerboodle: SPaG quizzes
   ◊ Kerboodle: Grammar reference guide

Note that the source texts and activities in *Catapult Workbook 1* can also be used as assessment material, if students haven't already used them to consolidate their learning from the Student Book.

# Chapter 6:
# Arguments and essays

## Chapter overview

### Why are we teaching this?

Understanding how writers present arguments and consider different viewpoints is a fundamental skill that all students need to acquire. By exploring high-quality texts, selected to be accessible and appealing, students can then develop their own writing skills through carefully supported activities.

Across the four units and in the final assessment in this chapter, students will read a range of non-fiction texts all relating to human relationships with animals. Texts include a poem about a caged tiger, an expository essay about the ethics of zoos, an argument against keeping snakes from PETA's website, a 19th-century extract about Jumbo the elephant kept at London Zoo and a narrative essay about a rhino on the verge of extinction. Students are given the opportunity to use the skills and techniques they have studied in these extracts in the writing assessment at the end of the chapter.

Many activities in this chapter will benefit from discussion prior to students completing a written response. Encourage students to elaborate and explain clearly their views and arguments. Speaking and listening skills are important prerequisites to developing effective reading and writing skills, so they should be an integral part of each unit.

### What are the learning aims?

In every unit in this chapter, students will learn to strengthen the core skills of:

- learning, understanding and practising using new vocabulary
- increasing general knowledge and contextual understanding.

In addition, each unit will focus on the following learning aims. Students will:

| Unit 1 | Unit 2 | Unit 3 | Unit 4 |
| --- | --- | --- | --- |
| • Show that they understand arguments from different writers.<br>• Explore how vocabulary and sentence structure can be used to express ideas and arguments.<br>• Learn, understand and practise using new vocabulary. | • Explore how information in a non-fiction text is presented and organised to support the text's purpose.<br>• Explore how writers use noun phrases, verbs, adjectives and punctuation to present arguments.<br>• Learn, understand and practise using new vocabulary. | • Make inferences from a 19th-century text, using evidence from the text to support their ideas.<br>• Explore how a writer selects words, phrases and sentence structures for effect, and use this skill in their own writing.<br>• Learn, understand and practise using new vocabulary. | • Identify the form and features of narrative essays.<br>• Explore a writer's techniques, such as the use of descriptive noun phrases, to produce an emotional response.<br>• Learn, understand and practise using new vocabulary. |

### How will this chapter be assessed?

The writing assessment at the end of the chapter gives students two different tasks for writing based on the skills practised through the units. There is clear guidance for planning with suggested criteria for inclusion in each piece.

Depending on the writing task chosen, the focuses for assessment will include some of the following:

- a lively description of an animal
- an anecdote relating to a pet
- rhetorical questions
- advice to pet owners
- factual information and statistics
- predicted counter-arguments and a prepared response
- appropriate sentence construction, using commas to separate clauses and phrases
- target words explored in the chapter.

Note that the short 'Check your skills' feature at the end of every unit in this chapter provides formative assessment opportunities to support the students' learning.

## Chapter 6 unit sequence

The sequence of units is designed so that students gain in confidence as they complete more challenging activities while progressing through the chapter.

Note that some activities feature in just the Teacher Book (TB).

<table>
<tr><td colspan="3">Chapter 6:<br>Arguments and essays</td></tr>
<tr><td></td><td>Student Book</td><td>Workbook</td></tr>
<tr>
<td>1: Freedom and captivity</td>
<td>Source texts: 'Tiger' by Leslie Norris and 'Zoos do a good job'
<ul>
<li>Discuss a confrontation with a wild animal and/or a visit to a zoo or safari park. (TB)</li>
<li>Analyse the use of language in the texts, which describe the tiger's state of mind (poem) and the arguments for zoos (extract).</li>
<li>Practise using specific vocabulary from/related to the texts.</li>
<li>Understand some techniques for writing an expository/argument essay.</li>
<li>Develop an argument against zoos in opposition to the points made in the source extract.</li>
</ul></td>
<td>Source text: 'Think twice before voting against animal circuses' by Douglas McPherson
<ul>
<li>Identify arguments and counter-arguments.</li>
<li>Write a letter to present arguments about banning animals in circuses.</li>
</ul></td>
</tr>
<tr>
<td>2: Reptile alert</td>
<td>Source text: '5 Reasons NEVER to Buy a Snake' by Jennifer O'Connor
<ul>
<li>Discuss the general image of the snake and whether or not snakes should ever be kept as pets. (TB)</li>
<li>Analyse the use of language that makes an emotive case for not keeping snakes as pets in a domestic environment.</li>
<li>Summarise a portion of the text to focus on the key points and ideas.</li>
<li>Explain how the writer has used information and deployed language to make a powerful argument against keeping snakes as pets.</li>
</ul></td>
<td>Source text: Extract from RSPCA website about keeping exotic pets
<ul>
<li>Analyse the structure and presentation of advice.</li>
<li>Explore effective noun phrases.</li>
</ul></td>
</tr>
<tr>
<td>3: Animal superstar</td>
<td>Source text: Extract from Autobiography of Matthew Scott, Jumbo's Keeper by Matthew Scott
<ul>
<li>Discuss the treatment of elephants and how much charities are working to help them survive. (TB)</li>
<li>Analyse the use of some unfamiliar language, then use it in writing to demonstrate understanding of meaning.</li>
<li>Collaborate on answering questions about language, using evidence in support of ideas.</li>
<li>Write a letter to London Zoo in the style of a Victorian.</li>
</ul></td>
<td>Source text: Extract from Wild Nature Won by Kindness by Elizabeth Brightwen
<ul>
<li>Draw inferences from the writer's language.</li>
<li>Write a letter demonstrating feelings through choice of language.</li>
</ul></td>
</tr>
</table>

<table>
<tr><td colspan="3" align="center">Chapter 6:<br>Arguments and essays</td></tr>
</table>

| | Student Book | Workbook |
|---|---|---|
| **4: An old warrior** | **Source text:** Extract from 'A picture of loneliness: you are looking at the last male northern white rhino' by Jonathan Jones<br><br>• Discuss what students would do if they knew a specific animal was about to become extinct. (TB)<br>• Explore the use of target words and look at how different word classes affect sentence structure.<br>• Analyse a reference chain of negativity used to emphasise the pessimism of the article.<br>• Explain how the writer uses specific stylistic features to make the reader feel sad for the last male northern white rhino. | **Source text:** Extract from 'Shooting an elephant' by George Orwell<br><br>• Explore techniques the writer uses to express views and inspire a reaction.<br>• Write a piece of advice putting forward arguments for a line of action. |
| **Writing assessment** | **Task:** select one of two writing tasks, either a narrative or expository essay about keeping pets<br><br>• Students are encouraged to include stylistic and structural features such as imagery, rhetorical questions, anecdotes and advice in the narrative essay.<br>• Information is given to support students writing the expository essay with a series of facts, statistics and opinions. | |

# Preparing to teach

## Refresh your knowledge

You might find it helpful to refer to the following key points when planning the teaching of this chapter.

Students should become familiar with reading and writing both expository and narrative essays, although knowledge of these actual terms is not essential.

**Expository essays** can investigate a topic, explain something with facts, describe a process or weigh up evidence both for and against something in a balanced manner and present an argument in a clear, concise manner. A classic expository essay is made up of five sections:

- an introductory paragraph that contains the thesis or main idea
- three further sections that make up the main body of the essay, giving details to support the thesis
- a concluding paragraph that restates the main idea and ties together the main points of the essay.

**Narrative essays** tell a story based on fact rather than fiction. The story is likely to include anecdotes and personal experiences, and follow a sequence of events linked by cause and effect. A narrative essay is likely to contain an overall point or relay a particular viewpoint, drawing out why a particular experience is significant.

Other forms of texts, such as articles and autobiographies, share many of the same features as the essays above.

## Links and further reading

- 'The Jaguar' by Ted Hughes is an excellent poem to compare with 'Tiger'. Students will see the parallels between Jones's perspective of the trapped predator and Hughes's portrayal of the animal dreaming about its natural habitat while pacing the narrow confines of its cage.
- Freedom for Animals is an organisation that campaigns to keep wild animals in their natural habitats rather than confining them for public entertainment. Their website can be found at: www.freedomforanimals.org.uk.
- The World Association of Zoos and Aquariums (WAZA) promotes what are seen as the positive aspects of keeping animals 'safe', with the slogan 'United for Conservation'. Their website can found at: http://www.waza.org/en/site/home.
- 'Understanding the motivations of beginner reptile owners' is a report published by the RSPCA. It gives detailed analysis of why so many reptiles are bought to be kept domestically and often die prematurely: https://www.rspca.org.uk/webContent/staticImages/Downloads/ReptileReport.pdf.
- The Pet Health Network advocates for the keeping of exotic pets and the website http://www.pethealthnetwork.com/all-pet-health/small-animal-health-care/why-choose-exotic-pet-anyway lists the benefits of keeping them from an owner's perspective.
- In addition to the biography of Matthew Scott, a large number of books have been written about Jumbo. *Jumbo: The Unauthorised Biography of a Victorian Sensation* by John Sutherland and *Jumbo – The Greatest Elephant in the World* by Paul Chambers both explore the tragic history of Jumbo and the attitudes towards animals that tolerated/allowed his treatment.
- In addition to the northern white rhino, there are a large number of animals facing extinction in the near future. Details of these have been collected on one website, which gives a full picture of the threat to the different species and some of the specific reasons: http://saveanimalsfacingextinction.org/.
- 'The greatest threat to people is ignorance. The greatest threat to animals is ignorant people.' This is a banner quotation for an e-book advocating the case for the ethical treatment of animals. Find it at: http://www.animalethics.org.uk/zoos.html.
- The article 'What is the point of saving endangered species?' very artfully poses all the questions people may have about the value of saving all species of animals from extinction: http://www.bbc.co.uk/earth/story/20150715-why-save-an-endangered-species

## Planning guidance and teaching tips

Think about how you can make the materials relevant to your students and responsive to their particular needs and learning targets. Some suggested approaches to address key areas are provided below.

- Encourage students to read widely, including a range of controversial topics, and to consider different perspectives of an argument. Students need to develop an awareness that different sides of a debate can and do give plausible arguments, but that an individual can appreciate elements of both sides without becoming an advocate for either.
- Ensure that all students have appropriate opportunities to speak, developing confidence in themselves and modelling higher levels of tolerance and patience with others, even those they disagree with.
- Refer to the Grammar reference guide on Kerboodle for definitions and examples of specific grammatical features covered by this chapter. Kerboodle also provides quizzes to help improve the technical accuracy of students' writing and the application of grammar in context.

# Unit focus

## Preparation and resources

- Student Book 1: pages 148–153
- Workbook 1: pages 48–49
- Kerboodle resources:
  - ◇ 6.1 Tiger audio
  - ◇ 6.1 Zoos do a good job audio
  - ◇ 6.1 Tiger quiz
  - ◇ 6.1 Zoos do a good job quiz
  - ◇ 6.1 Word power worksheet
  - ◇ 6.1 Effective argument worksheet
- Grammatical knowledge: adjective, phrase
- Key terms: adjective, expository essay, phrase, sentence structure, stanza, verb

## What this unit teaches and how

- The unit uses two writers' views about zoos: the poem 'Tiger' by Leslie Norris and an essay 'Zoos do a good job'. The activities explore how vocabulary and sentence structure support the delivery of arguments in an effective expository essay. Students are given the opportunity to write a paragraph for another expository essay.

- *Catapult Workbook 1* supports and develops the skills in this lesson through analysing an article about using animals in circuses 'Think twice before voting against animal circuses' by Douglas McPherson, which featured in *The Telegraph*.

## Skills and objectives

In this unit, students will:

- Show that they understand arguments from different writers.

- Explore how vocabulary and sentence structure can be used to express ideas and arguments.

- Learn, understand and practise using new vocabulary.

# Teaching suggestions and guidance

This unit is designed to cover two to three lessons, depending on the ability level of your students and the length of lesson time.

## Introduction to the unit (p148)

- Ask students to describe a time when they came face to face with an animal or bird in the wild. It may have been an urban or rural encounter. Encourage descriptions of the animal's appearance, behaviour and reactions to the observer.

- Discuss what students think about the way animals are kept in zoos and safari parks. Gather feedback and identify the range of feelings.

## Engaging with the source texts (p149)

- Read the poem 'Tiger' with a suitable backdrop image of a tiger looking trapped and forlorn – ideally looking through bars, e.g. http://www.dailymail.co.uk/news/article-2525402/Zookeeper-mauled-death-rare-tiger-cleaned-enclosure-Shanghai-animal-park.html. Choose an appropriate image for reading 'Zoos do a good job'.

- Alternatively, play the audio recordings of the poem and text on Kerboodle: 6.1 Tiger audio and 6.1 Zoos do a good job audio.

- Take feedback on the 'Ready, set, go!' task, encouraging students to identify relevant words and phrases.

- To test basic comprehension of the poem and text, ask students to complete the 6.1 Tiger quiz and 6.1 Zoos do a good job quiz on Kerboodle. These can be completed as a whole-class activity or individually.

**Resources**

- ◇ Kerboodle: 6.1 Tiger audio and 6.1 Zoos do a good job audio
- ◇ Kerboodle: 6.1 Tiger quiz and 6.1 Zoos do a good job quiz

## Word power (pp150–151)

- For Activity 1, it may help to use the image of a tiger behind bars to juxtapose the 'living' colourful stripes of the animal and the dark metal bars.

- Support students with Activity 2 by offering vocabulary such as: stealth, predator.

- For Activity 3, support students' reasoning with ideas such as observation giving opportunities to scrutinise, analyse and learn.

- Support students with exemplars for Activity 6, such as:

  ◊ … he is in demand in the local area.
  ◊ … it is a skill that is in demand.

- Use the 6.1 Word power worksheet on Kerboodle to reinforce and develop the target words covered in this unit.

**Resources**
◊ Kerboodle: 6.1 Word power worksheet

## Knowledge and understanding (p152)

- For Activity 1, support students by asking which of the following quotations is more appropriate in answer to the question: 'few steps' or 'concrete cell'.

- For Activity 2, ensure students are familiar with the term 'stanza'. To check, ask them how many stanzas are in the 'Tiger' poem (five).

- Use the following phrases to support students in their responses to Activity 3: the tiger's instinct; in its natural state/habitat; being restricted from normal behaviour/nature.

## Writing skills (pp152–153)

- For Activity 1, support students with clear definitions of words and their meanings in context, e.g. the way that 'stalks' relates to the natural behaviour of a wild predator. For the 'wild/zoo' part of the question, offer the juxtaposition of free/natural with confined/unnatural.

- Activity 2 may be more difficult for some students due to the reference to 'cruel', but offer an alternative phrasing, e.g. animals are <u>in danger of extinction</u>; zoos are a necessary way to protect animals <u>from extinction</u>.

- Use the 6.1 Effective argument worksheet on Kerboodle to give students the opportunity to reinforce their understanding of how to anticipate and counter possible opposing arguments.

**Resources**
◊ Kerboodle: 6.1 Effective argument worksheet

## Check your skills (p153)

- If necessary, revise previous writing where students have had to present an argument and support points of view with evidence.

- Support students in meeting the criteria for features that should be included in their paragraph. The following ideas may be helpful for presenting an argument and counter-arguments using impersonal constructions:

  ◊ Some scientists may explain that… but it can also be argued that…
  ◊ Freedom is a right for humans, so why can't…
  ◊ Although zoos are popular with people… the animals…
  ◊ We are not helping animals by… we are in fact…

- Include opportunities for peer-assessment during the writing process. Ask students whether they are convinced by the argument – and if not, why not?

# Unit focus

## Preparation and resources

- Student Book 1: pages 154–159
- Workbook 1: pages 50–51
- Kerboodle resources:
  ◊ 6.2 5 Reasons NEVER to Buy a Snake audio
  ◊ 6.2 5 Reasons NEVER to Buy a Snake quiz
  ◊ 6.2 Word power worksheet
  ◊ 6.2 Anecdote worksheet
- Grammatical knowledge: noun, noun phrase
- Key terms: anecdote, non-fiction, noun (WB), noun phrase, subheading, summary

## What this unit teaches and how

- This unit focuses on the extract '5 Reasons NEVER to Buy a Snake', based on a PETA (People for the Ethical Treatment of Animals) online article. The writer makes a strong argument against people acquiring snakes as pets. The activities explore how the presentation of the text supports the text's purpose and examines the use of vocabulary and punctuation to make the argument effective.

- *Catapult Workbook 1* supports and develops the skills in this unit through an extract from the RSPCA website, which gives detailed advice on what to consider before acquiring exotic pets (including snakes).

## Skills and objectives

In this unit, students will:

- Explore how information in a non-fiction text is presented and organised to support the text's purpose.

- Explore how writers use noun phrases, verbs, adjectives and punctuation to present arguments.

- Learn, understand and practise using new vocabulary.

# Teaching suggestions and guidance

This unit is designed to cover two to three lessons, depending on the ability level of your students and the length of lesson time.

### Introduction to the unit (p154)

- Project an image of a snake on the IWB. Ask students to work in groups to collect words and phrases that represent thoughts and feelings about snakes. Gather feedback, drawing out ideas such as snakes are evil, predatory, dangerous, sly, charming, furtive, poisonous, elegant, fascinating, etc.

- Ask whether anyone owns a snake. Discuss possible positive and negative reasons for owning a snake. Try to arrive at a consensus as to whether it is a good or bad idea, and the dominant reason for arriving at this conclusion.

### Engaging with the source text (p155)

- Read the text with the students or play the audio recording from Kerboodle: 6.2 5 Reasons NEVER to Buy a Snake audio.

- Give students a copy of the text – or project it in front of the class – and ask them to highlight any words that they feel are 'emotive' (stir up the readers' emotions). Do not define any particular emotion at this stage.

- Take feedback from the 'Ready, set, go!' task, looking at the organisation of the text. Draw out the value of dividing up the text like this to make it accessible and for ease of identifying particular arguments.

- To test basic comprehension of the extract, ask students to complete the 6.2 5 Reasons NEVER to Buy a Snake quiz on Kerboodle. This can be completed as a whole-class activity or individually.

**Resources**
◊ Kerboodle: 6.2 5 Reasons NEVER to Buy a Snake audio
◊ Kerboodle: 6.2 5 Reasons NEVER to Buy a Snake quiz

## Word power (p156)

- In response to Activity 2, students may refer to the fact that the text says that snakes don't like being handled or touched by humans. Encourage students to think further about this, maybe concluding that snakes are solitary animals in the wild, so don't seek company, or may be afraid of humans.

- For Activity 4, the literal answer in the text is 'lush jungles and swamps'. However, ask students to express this differently, e.g. space away from urban areas; open space filled with trees; places with lots of vegetation.

- Ensure that in Activity 5, students understand that the phrase 'Sky-high mortality' is an example of visual imagery. The purpose of this visual image is to exaggerate the death rate for emphasis and to make the argument more dramatic and powerful.

- Use the 6.2 Word power worksheet on Kerboodle to reinforce and develop students' confidence with the emotive vocabulary used in the source text in this unit.

### Resources
◇ Kerboodle: 6.2 Word power worksheet

## Knowledge and understanding (p157)

- The activities in this section often require answers with an explanation (rather than just word identification), so it may benefit students to work in pairs to discuss their responses before they write them down.

- For Activity 2, ask students to suggest alternative ways of expressing 'keeping an eye open'. Gather ideas and draw out suggestions such as: being wary, alert, on guard.

- For Activity 5, set a limit of 15 words for the summary. Collect the summaries on sticky notes at the front of the room to share.

## Reading skills (pp158-159)

- To reinforce students' understanding of anecdotes and to develop their ability to write their own, use the 6.2 Anecdote worksheet on Kerboodle.

- For Activity 1, guide students towards understanding that by including an anecdote about herself, the writer has personalised the article and gained the reader's interest before developing the more formal argument against keeping snakes.

- In Activity 2b, guide students towards 'replacement'. Discuss whether both words ('pet' and 'replacement') effectively reduce the animal to a disposable material commodity. This could encourage the defence of having pets, but remind students that the argument is not about all pets.

- Activity 3 gives students a chance to make lexical links in both subject and tone. Suggest 'cruel' and 'dirty' to encourage debate and deeper thinking.

### Resources
◇ Kerboodle: 6.2 Anecdote worksheet

## Check your skills (p159)

- If necessary, remind students how to integrate evidence from the text in the form of quotations or paraphrasing.

- Some students may benefit from discussing ideas before they write their response, e.g. identifying powerful verbs and adjectives could be done collaboratively. (Remind them how to identify verbs and adjectives if necessary.)

- If students need support in structuring their sentences, offer some of the following models:

  ◇ The writer has selected some… subheadings to help persuade…
  ◇ When the writer states that… percent of…, this emphasises…
  ◇ The life of a snake as a pet is portrayed as… through words such as…
  ◇ The…, … and… treatment of snakes is illustrated by…

# Unit focus

## Preparation and resources

- Student Book 1: pages 160–165
- Workbook 1: pages 52–53
- Kerboodle resources:
  - ◊ 6.3 Autobiography of Matthew Scott, Jumbo's Keeper audio
  - ◊ 6.3 Autobiography of Matthew Scott, Jumbo's Keeper quiz
  - ◊ 6.3 Word power worksheet
  - ◊ 6.3 Contrast worksheet
- Grammatical knowledge: clause
- Key terms: autobiography, clause, contrast, inference, metaphor, rhythm

## What this unit teaches and how

- This unit focuses on an extract from the 19th-century text *Autobiography of Matthew Scott, Jumbo's Keeper* by Matthew Scott. The activities guide students in how to make inferences, drawing on evidence from the text. Students also explore how to use vocabulary and sentence structures effectively in their own writing.

- *Catapult Workbook 1* supports and develops the skills in this unit through an extract from *Wild Nature Won By Kindness* by Elizabeth Brightwen (1898).

## Skills and objectives

In this unit, students will:

- Make inferences from a 19th-century text, using evidence from the text to support their ideas.

- Explore how a writer selects words, phrases and sentence structures for effect, and use this skill in their own writing.

- Learn, understand and practise using new vocabulary.

# Teaching suggestions and guidance

This unit is designed to cover two to three lessons, depending on the ability level of your students and the length of lesson time.

## Introduction to the unit (p160)

- Discuss how elephants have been hunted historically for their ivory tusks, putting them in danger of extinction. Ensure students understand that 'trophy hunting' is a hotly debated issue and that bans are now in place to try to conserve elephants, although the hunting still continues in places.

- Discuss the fact that very few people in Europe had ever seen an elephant until Victorian times and, even then, only a limited number could have seen Jumbo at London Zoo. Give students some brief information about the establishment of 'zoos', e.g.:

  - ◊ The collecting of wild animals foreign to the UK was begun by William the Conqueror, who kept a royal menagerie, symbolising the power of royalty. Future monarchs were given further exotic animals as gifts and the collection grew.
  - ◊ Elizabeth I was the first monarch to allow the public to see the royal menagerie at the Tower of London, as long as they brought dead cats and dogs with which to feed the animals.
  - ◊ The first travelling zoo was established in 1839 by George Wombwell when he realised that people would pay to see the animals.

## Engaging with the source text (p161)

- Read the extract with an image of Jumbo on the IWB. The tone of the text is intentionally sentimental and designed to not only give a positive image of the captive elephant, but also the keeper.

- Alternatively, play the audio recording of the extract on Kerboodle: 6.3 Autobiography of Matthew Scott, Jumbo's Keeper audio.

- Take feedback from the 'Ready, set, go!' task. If necessary, focus the students' attention on words in the first paragraph, such as 'nursed', 'baby', 'father', 'mother', 'my boy'. Draw out that such terms convey a sense of the keeper's protective, affectionate attitude towards Jumbo.

- To test basic comprehension of the extract, ask students to complete the 6.3 Autobiography of Matthew Scott, Jumbo's Keeper quiz on

Kerboodle. This can be completed as a whole-class activity or individually.

**Resources**
◊ Kerboodle: 6.3 Autobiography of Matthew Scott, Jumbo's Keeper audio
◊ Kerboodle: 6.3 Autobiography of Matthew Scott, Jumbo's Keeper quiz

## Word power (pp162–163)

- For Activity 2, gather a range of words that reference the slow progress of the elephant, such as: stately, slowly, methodically. Ask students what else is often referred to as a 'procession' (a wedding or funeral).

- The word 'engaged' in Activity 3 will be easily linked to a proposal of marriage but some students may not have met the term as meaning that someone is already on the phone when a call is made.

- In Activity 4, most students will understand the meaning of 'deliberately' in the sense of 'on purpose' but may not have heard the word used in the sense of 'slowly and carefully'. Discuss how 'deliberate' (verb) can be used in a similar way to mean 'think deeply and/or at length' before making a decision.

- Use the 6.3 Word power worksheet on Kerboodle to reinforce students' understanding of the target words in this unit.

**Resources**
◊ Kerboodle: 6.3 Word power worksheet

## Knowledge and understanding (p164)

- All the questions in this section demand evidence from the text or an interpretation. Set the students to work in groups of three to collaborate and agree on the answers.

- Give a minute for one member from the group to share two answers with another group (the choice must be made before the visits). Groups can then make any changes in the light of any new information.

- Gather feedback and expect students to give their answers in the style and structure of a written sentence using accurate evidence.

## Writing skills (pp164–165)

- For Activity 1a, guide students towards the adjectives. These can be stressed when spoken aloud as if underlined or emboldened.

- For Activity 1d, ask students to work in pairs to write the sentence using the 'rule of three'. If necessary, model the following example:

  ◊ She was the tallest, strongest and most athletic of the players in the team.

- For Activity 2a and b, students should arrive at impressions such as:

  ◊ Jumbo: sensitive, caring, protective
  ◊ Mother: anxious, shocked, overwhelmed

- For Activity 2c, set a limit of 50 words for the brief paragraph explaining how Scott uses language to show contrast. If necessary, offer the following sentence starter for support:

  ◊ The use of the adverbs 'gently' and 'tenderly' shows that…

- Use the 6.3 Contrast worksheet on Kerboodle to reinforce and support students' understanding of the use of contrast in writing.

**Resources**
◊ Kerboodle: 6.3 Contrast worksheet

## Check your skills (p165)

- For the Victorian-style letter begging London Zoo not to sell Jumbo, support students with the following suggested starters:

  ◊ How can you consider the sale of 'our boy' Jumbo when he is so…
  ◊ Shame on you, sirs! It is impossible to allow the desire for money to…
  ◊ The gentle giant, the heroic child-saviour, the jewel of London Zoo…
  ◊ We beg of you, sirs, do not do this…
  ◊ How can you have this dreadful deed on your consciences? We demand that…

- If necessary, remind students how to include a quotation in the text, using correct punctuation.

- Encourage students to swap the first draft of their letters and proofread them for errors, before returning them and writing their final drafts.

# Unit focus

## Preparation and resources

- Student Book 1: pages 166–171
- Workbook 1: pages 54–55
- Kerboodle resources:
  - ◇ 6.4 A picture of loneliness audio
  - ◇ 6.4 A picture of loneliness quiz
  - ◇ 6.4 Word power worksheet
  - ◇ 6.4 Emotive language worksheet
- Grammatical knowledge: adverb
- Key terms: adverb, emotive language (WB), modal verb (WB), narrative essay, rhetorical question

## What this unit teaches and how

- This unit focuses on an extract from 'A picture of loneliness: you are looking at the last male northern white rhino', a thought-provoking description of the plight of this last rhino. Through the activities, students analyse some of the features of a narrative essay and the use of emotive language.

- *Catapult Workbook 1* supports and develops the skills in this unit through an extract from 'Shooting an elephant' by George Orwell. Students identify some of the stylistic features used within the text and comment on their effect.

## Skills and objectives

In this unit, students will:

- Identify the form and features of narrative essays.

- Explore a writer's techniques, such as the use of descriptive noun phrases, to produce an emotional response.

- Learn, understand and practise using new vocabulary.

# Teaching suggestions and guidance

This unit is designed to cover two to three lessons, depending on the ability level of your students and the length of lesson time.

## Introduction to the unit (p166)

- Ask students what they would do if they knew a specific animal was about to become extinct. Working in pairs, ask them to come up with three key action points. Gather feedback, then discuss what might actually make a difference and agree on five key points.

- Develop the discussion to further consider how to stop such a situation ever happening. How would the action points be put into practice? Would there have to be rewards as well as sanctions?

## Engaging with the source text (p167)

- Create a slideshow depicting the northern white rhino. Start with pictures of many rhinos and gradually diminish the numbers in the images before ending it with a picture of Sudan standing alone with his guards. Read the text while the images change. Alternatively, play the audio recording of the extract on Kerboodle: 6.4 A picture of loneliness audio.

- Take feedback from the 'Ready, set, go!' task. Draw out the emotions evoked by words and phrases such as 'on the planet', 'lovingly guarded', 'brutality', 'hack off', 'precious', 'sad black dot', 'vulnerable', 'old warrior', 'fading'.

- To test basic comprehension of the extract, ask students to complete the 6.4 A picture of loneliness quiz on Kerboodle. This can be completed as a whole-class activity or individually.

**Resources**
- ◇ Kerboodle: 6.4 A picture of loneliness audio
- ◇ Kerboodle: 6.4 A picture of loneliness quiz

## Word power (pp168-169)

- For Activity 1, to develop the students' understanding, ask them to create a noun from 'vigilant' and to use it accurately in a sentence, e.g. vigilance or vigil – The guards have to demonstrate great <u>vigilance</u> to ensure that Sudan remains safe and protected.

- For Activity 3b, support students with ideas for the 'melancholy scene' with the following ideas:

  ◇ someone who has received bad news: shocked, forlorn, helpless, lost
  ◇ the scene of a funeral: tearful, sorrow, loss, emptiness.

- To develop Activity 4, explain the usually negative use of 'fateful' (e.g. as a signal of doom). Ask students to use the word 'fateful' accurately in sentences that show both its serious and more light-hearted application. Support them with the following examples if required:

  ◇ On that fateful day, she made a decision that would haunt her for years.
  ◇ I asked my mum that fateful question: 'Are we nearly there yet?'

- Use the 6.4 Word power worksheet on Kerboodle to reinforce students' understanding of the vocabulary used in the source text for this unit, including the target words and adverbs.

**Resources**
◇ Kerboodle: 6.4 Word power worksheet

## Knowledge and understanding (p169)

- For Activity 4, the first part should provoke some interesting answers. Collect these on sticky notes at the front of the room and share the ideas, e.g. he will die alone; childless.

- Most students should select 'pessimistic' for the overall tone of the article. Refer to the reference chain of negative words and phrases in the text to support students' ideas, e.g. 'last'; 'does not mate'; 'no more of their kind'; 'slim chance'.

## Reading skills (pp170-171)

- To extend Activity 2, ask students to think of an alternative but just as powerfully effective rhetorical question to begin the article. Ask them for another to end it, such as:

  ◇ So – do we just stand by, shed a tear and watch?
  ◇ When he is dead, which species will be next?

- If students need more guidance for Activity 3, point out that the guards and their guns are protecting Sudan but represent a resistance to the threat of 'brutality' from poachers. Ask them to explain how it can be argued that it is a picture of love. Draw out ideas such as: guarding, nurturing, protecting, sheltering from harm, etc.

- Use the 6.4 Emotive language worksheet on Kerboodle to explore and reinforce students' understanding of how writers trigger an emotional response in readers. This worksheet also considers the use of rhetorical questions.

**Resources**
◇ Kerboodle: 6.4 Emotive language worksheet

## Check your skills (p171)

- Set a maximum of 75 words for this task. Support students with the following sentence starters if required:

  ◇ A strong animal is described as 'vulnerable' so that the reader…
  ◇ The use of the words 'majestic' and 'noble' shows that…
  ◇ His skin is metaphorically referred to as 'armour', which shows…

# Assessment suggestions and guidance

## Why are we assessing this?

Students have completed the chapter on Arguments and essays, exploring these aspects through a variety of high-quality contemporary, 20th- and pre-20th-century texts. The units have reinforced and developed the essential reading and writing skills outlined below, consolidating knowledge and increasing students' confidence.

This assessment unit gives students and teachers the opportunity to assess and reflect on how firmly these skills – in particular, the writing skills – have been grasped and how effectively students can employ them in an assessment situation.

## What are students demonstrating?

Students are asked to write either a narrative or an expository essay, including some of the features listed below (depending on which option they choose):

- a lively description of an animal
- an anecdote relating to a pet
- rhetorical questions
- advice to pet owners
- factual information and statistics
- predicted counter-arguments and a prepared response
- appropriate sentence construction, using commas to separate clauses and phrases
- target words explored in the chapter.

## How to deliver the assessment

- Being asked to produce extended writing texts under pressure of time is one of the most difficult expectations of students. You will need to judge the level of support required for individuals and the whole class. All students should feel that they are able to complete the task with some confidence and skill before they start.
- The tasks can be completed in one sitting or could be split into sections. For maximum support, this could mean that each paragraph can be attempted based on the inclusion of particular criteria. This staged approach is formulaic but will build confidence of weaker students as they see their skills develop.

- Students could be given a free choice or all work on the same titles to enable whole-class planning and preparation. Depending on the group, you could use peer-assessment so students can receive some feedback before submitting the final text for formal assessment.
- Use some or all of the following sentence starters to support students in planning and writing:

### Task 1 (Narrative essay)

- ◊ The loyalty of my smooth-haired guardian…
- ◊ Panting enthusiastically as she ran clumsily towards…
- ◊ Falling down a bank covered in thorn bushes was not exactly…
- ◊ Who could ask for a better companion than… ?
- ◊ The golden rule for instilling good behaviour in your pet is that…

### Task 2 (Expository essay)

- ◊ A staggering statistic that shows the popularity of… is that…
- ◊ The public feel that to be an owner…, people should…
- ◊ Some people may well argue that…, however, …
- ◊ On the other hand, it is clear that…
- ◊ We know that a lot of money is spent on pets because…
- ◊ Unfortunately, some owners 'treat' their pets too much because…

## How to mark the assessment

You will want to mark this in line with departmental and school marking guidelines. If you wish, you could use the *Catapult* marking scales (provided on Kerboodle). The *Catapult* marking scales are designed to assess lower-attaining students who need to consolidate skills that have not yet been fully grasped but need to be secured and developed in order to move those students forward and narrow the gap between their existing levels of achievement and national expectations for KS3.

Using the *Catapult* marking scales will help you to identify specific strengths and areas for improvement in an individual student's writing. This may help you to set development targets as well as building a profile of your class as writers.

## Following up the assessment

The assessment should enable you to identify clear areas in which students have underperformed and you can therefore plan in detail how to reinforce understanding using *Catapult* resources.

1. Refer to the *Catapult* mapping grids on pages 132-135 of this Teacher Book to identify other *Catapult* chapters where these reading and writing skills are covered. For example:

   ◇ rhetorical questions are also covered in Chapter 4 (Unit 2)
   ◇ advice texts are also covered in Chapter 4 (Unit 4).

2. Direct students to the SPaG quizzes on Kerboodle to address any areas of weakness that the assessment may have revealed. For example, basic skills can be reinforced with the following quizzes:

   ◇ Inverted commas for quotations
   ◇ Questions
   ◇ Exclamations
   ◇ Commas.

   Encourage students to proofread their work, looking for ways of making their writing style more concise and fluent. For example, skills can be reinforced with the following quizzes:

   ◇ Noun phrases
   ◇ Adverbials
   ◇ Adjectives
   ◇ Adverbs
   ◇ Conjunctions
   ◇ Parenthesis
   ◇ Verbs and tenses.

The Grammar reference guide on Kerboodle contains definitions and additional examples of each of the spelling, punctuation and grammar points covered in the quizzes, for your reference.

3. If the students' vocabulary seems limited, remind them to make use of the target words they have explored, which are also contained in the target word list at the back of the Student Book. Students may also benefit from compiling their own vocabulary lists for reference. These should be shared and discussed regularly.

### Resources
◇ Kerboodle: *Catapult* marking scales
◇ Kerboodle: SPaG quizzes
◇ Kerboodle: Grammar reference guide

Note that the source texts and activities in *Catapult Workbook 1* can also be used as assessment material, if students haven't already used them to consolidate their learning from the Student Book.

# Student Book 1 Answers
## Chapter 1: Characters and setting

## Unit 1: First impressions

*Pages 6–11*

### Word power

1. **a.** cautiously
   **b.** quickly
   **c.** carefully
3. **a.** Answers should include reference to the idea that there was a great deal of dust and that it was moving.
   **b.** Answers should include reference to the idea that the dust was so thick that it almost stopped him breathing or that the dust was in the air.
4. **a.** 'He <u>was covered</u> in dust and webs like everything else …'.
   **b.** Answers should include reference to the idea that every part of the garage was dusty, including the man.
5. **a.** My heart <u>thudded</u> and <u>thundered</u>.
   **b.** Answers should include reference to the sound that his heart made (repeated 'th') and how this conveys his state of alarm effectively or how it represents repeated loud heartbeats.
6. Answers will vary. Look for answers that show a good awareness of the viewpoint of the narrator as he or she explores the room. Strong answers will include all the success criteria and will be carefully paced to create tension, focusing on description rather than action. Weaker answers may feel rushed or contain too many sudden events.

### Knowledge and understanding

1. This implies that he was plucking up his courage because his parents had forbidden him to enter the garage and he could hear scratching – both of these made him nervous.
2. The scratching came from a corner of the garage.
3. He saw a million woodlice scattering away.
4. He found the bones of some little animal that had died in there.
5. Furniture, newspapers and magazines
6. Answers will vary. Students might choose the old newspapers, the dust or the undisturbed cobwebs plus a relevant explanation.

### Reading skills

**a. and b.** Students should select the following (all with suitable explanations):

- 'head tipped back'
- 'covered in dust and webs'
- covered in dead bluebottles.

### Check your skills

Students should weave their notes from the previous task into a piece of continuous prose. A good answer will include all the success criteria and be coherent. Weaker answers may be a list of points without suitable linking words and phrases or may be lacking direct quotations.

## Unit 2: Flashback

*Pages 12–17*

### Word power

1. Line 2: verb – something moving in a motion like waves
   Final line: noun – a series of small waves
2. To slope
3. Gradual and cautious
4. Answers will vary.
5. Answers will vary, but should include reference to the idea that the sun has coloured the water below it in the same way that one coloured paint bleeds into another. Note: students may need help to form their answers. Encourage them to use words such as 'streaks' or 'drops'.
6. **a.** Jumping or diving. The word also implies force.

### Knowledge and understanding

1. She doesn't want to see Aunt Bev, Uncle Tom or her father.
2. Answers will vary. She goes to a smaller cove. She walks away from the coast path, towards the gorse at the edge of the cliff, and then climbs down the rocks to the cove.
3. **a.** Sample answer: 'Sometimes we'd wait for hours.'
   **b.** Explanations will vary, but should include the idea that she was happy to wait for the dolphins

with her mother because she knew they would eventually come.

4. Sample answer: 'They would rise up like magical creatures from another world…'
5. **a.** The day has nearly ended. The sun is setting.
   **b.** A dolphin leaps from the water.
   **c.** Answers may vary, but should include reference to the idea that her mother may be alive and attempting to communicate.

## Writing skills

1. The touch of the rock on her back
2. Students should identify the following: Kara hears the dolphins calling through the water, sees the sunlight shining from their backs, hears their breaths bursting above the water, sees them leap and somersault. Students may also identify 'she could feel them' as a 'sixth sense'.

## Check your skills

Answers will vary, but good answers should include all the success criteria, introducing the flashback clearly by changing tense and using a sensual trigger. Weaker answers my handle the flashback more clumsily – muddling the tenses or making the narrative difficult to follow.

# Unit 3: Under the surface

*Pages 18–23*

## Word power

1. Answers will vary, but should include reference to the idea that people were silent because they were shocked or worried, but also fascinated.
2. Answers will vary. Answers might include reference to the idea that 'bleating' describes a pathetic or pitiable sound, like a defenceless lamb.
3. To beat someone with a stick or whip
4. Answers will vary. Answers might include reference to the idea of the mud growing and billowing out like a flower blooming.
5. **a. and b.** Answers will vary.

## Knowledge and understanding

1. 'Drowned', 'blue-lipped', 'lay for dead'
2. **a.** Her mother is carrying out mouth to mouth resuscitation or the 'kiss of life'.

**b.** This implies that her mother did something courageous that no-one else did and the poet is proud of her actions.
3. **a.** Answers might include any of the following: for causing a fuss, to teach her not to play near water again.
   **b.** Cruel, harsh, poverty-stricken, violent

## Reading skills

1. The second quotation has already been explored in Word power activity 4. The third quotation gives the impression of turbulence, the surface being churned up by the swan's feet and wings.
2. The poem suggests that memory isn't reliable.

## Check your skills

A good answer will raise the issue of whether we can fully trust our memories and how Clarke explores this idea. Although the memory is detailed, could that detail have been invented? There is no way to know if it was. The reader, like Clarke, cannot decide. Weaker answers might come down on one side or the other.

# Unit 4: Imprisoned in the past

*Pages 24–29*

## Word power

1. Brightness
2. **a.** regret
   **b.** ghastly
   **c.** withered
3. **a.** Pip noticed that Miss Havisham's watch and the clock had been stopped at exactly the same time.
   **b.** He inferred that she had stopped the watch and clock at twenty to nine, the time when she was told that her marriage was cancelled.
4. Answers will vary.

## Knowledge and understanding

1. The bride (Miss Havisham) had withered, sunken eyes, shrunk to skin and bone. Pip also compares her to a waxwork of a dead body and refers to her as a skeleton.
2. Answers will vary, but students should show that they understand that on her wedding day she was young and beautiful, and her wedding dress was once white and her eyes glowing with happiness.

**3.** a – false, b – true, c – true , d – false, e – cannot be certain, f – true, g – false

## Reading skills

1. Waxworks look like people but they are objects, so she seemed to him not to be a living person.
2. He says 'I should have cried out' (make sure that students understand the archaic meaning of 'should'). He avoided her eyes. When she asks him if he is frightened of her, he lies and says 'no'.
3. Answers will vary. Ensure that students can re-create the wedding day and the effect it had on her, using evidence from the text to support their ideas.

## Check your skills

Ensure that students don't just repeat the factual events of the effects of the wedding day (e.g. she never left the house again), but explore the psychological effects of her experience (e.g. why she never left the house again). Strong answers may make references to mental breakdown and dramatic personality change.

# Unit 5: A test of character

*Pages 30–35*

## Word power

1. **a.** worrying
   **b.** with pleasure
   **c.** clear
2. **a.** Sample answer: throwing
   **b.** Sample answer: crowded with, full of, alive with
4. Green is also used to describe the look of someone about to be sick. He is feeling seasick.
5. Answers will vary.

## Knowledge and understanding

1. Four miles
2. Likely answers will include: Davie was seasick so he is not used to the sea; he is small; he is scared by the thought of climbing the Stac (accompanied by relevant quotations).
3. Kenneth is a bully ('the bully Kenneth'), who makes fun of Davie for being nervous and inexperienced.
4. **a.** John began to drum on the boards with his feet and the rest joined in.
   **b.** Mr Cane told them to stop their noise or they would 'wake every dead sailor from his resting place'. He frightened them into silence.

**5. B** Boreray
   **C** Stac Lee
   **D** Warrior Stac

## Reading skills

1. Rough, choppy, stormy
2. **a.** Answers may vary, but students are likely to choose Davie.
   **b.** Any quotation that refers to Davie's seasickness.
3. Answers may vary, but good ones should include: The use of the whale to indicate size and motion and the impression of height created by the image. Students should comment on the use of 'pitching' to indicate force and 'bulk' to indicate size. Strong answers may also refer to the threatening nature of the image ('aiming to swallow the moon').

## Check your skills

Answers will vary. Strong answers will pick out the metaphor from the previous task and the simile of the Devil's horn. They are also likely to include the repetition of 'so' and the comparison with Boreray. Points will be supported by short quotations. Weaker answers are likely to be less detailed.

# Unit 6: Reading assessment

*Pages 36–37*

1. A tunic with the three lions of Salisbury on a background of blue and gold, covering a chain-mail shirt.
2. Answers may vary but should include: "I cannot offer you a hand of flesh and blood", 'his chain mail shimmered', 'his features began to blur like a photograph that's out of focus. His whole body began to fade'. Each quotation should be explained fully.
3. **a.** Impressive, kind and sad
   **b.** Any of the above accompanied by a suitable quotation.
4. Answers will vary but a good answer should include many of the following:
   - Unhappy – seeking help
   - Imaginative and a dreamer – playing make-believe games to escape from his unhappiness when he was six
   - An absent father and bullied by older kids
   - Perhaps over-sensitive – frightened by storms
   - Frightened by the ghost but also pleased to see him. Perhaps a cure for his loneliness?
   - Feels sympathy for the ghost's unhappiness.

# Student Book 1 Answers
## Chapter 2: Action and atmosphere

## Unit 1: A dramatic opening

*Pages 38–43*

### Word power

1. **a.** (Groggily), the patient shook her head (groggily) as the doctor held the light in front of her eyes. (Groggily), the boxer stumbled (groggily) from the force of the blow.
   **b.** Answers will vary.
2. **a.** Shocking, outrageous or monster-like. Make sure that the student is aware that the size of the voice (e.g. loudness) is not being described.
   **b.** Her voice had a musical quality to it – <u>soft</u> and <u>melodious</u>, <u>low</u> and <u>haunting</u>, <u>warm</u> and <u>pure</u> – or any other appropriate combinations.
   His eyes had a robotic quality to them – <u>steely</u> and <u>cold</u>, <u>fixed</u> and <u>empty</u>, <u>hard</u> and <u>staring</u> – or any other appropriate combinations.
3. **a.** 'Straining' implies that he was trying very hard and had to listen intently in order to hear the voice.
   **b.** Answers will vary.
4. Answers will vary.

### Knowledge and understanding

1. Just after or at midnight
2. 'The one he'd been having a lot lately.'
3. His father does not live with the family. He speaks to Conor on the phone every two weeks. His dad is in America.
4. It wasn't a voice he recognised. It wasn't a woman's voice. It was unlikely to be his dad because he was in America. It didn't sound human (it sounded like a monster).

### Writing skills

1. Answers will vary. Students are unlikely to select 'happy', 'funny' or 'peaceful' but should be able to find evidence for the others.
2. Answers will vary.
3. **a.** Indicative content: Students should refer to Conor's fear or confusion causing him to question himself and to criticise himself for being scared. He is also trying to reassure himself.
   **b.** The monster only says Conor's name. It is the quality of the voice (unknown, monstrous) that frightens Conor.
4. **a.** Indicative content: Students should refer to the word 'rush' to describe the swift, sudden physical and involuntary effect of panic. The feeling of his guts being twisted is a metaphor describing what fear feels like physically. 'Twisting' creates quite a violent effect.
   **b.** The question refers to the fear in the nightmare (which might have contained a monster). He is frightened that his dream had become reality.
   **c.** Answers will vary. Students may refer to the use of dashes to indicate thoughts that Conor doesn't want to describe, the use of questions to indicate his confusion or the way he talks to himself for reassurance. They may pick out a sentence like 'Conor swallowed' to indicate fear.

### Check your skills

Answers will vary. Strong answers will maintain the 'voice' and tone of the original. The monster may also say more but still remain unknown.

## Unit 2: An unusual companion

*Pages 44–49*

### Word power

1. **a.** He was startled by Dracula's sudden hand on his shoulder when he hadn't seen him in the mirror.
   **b.** alarmed
2. **a.** Answers will vary. A good answer should include the idea that the feeling (unease) is mild and he is unsure why he feels this way. He feels the Count to be mildly threatening or that he feels tense when he is with him.
   **b.** He doesn't know why
   **c.** Answers will vary.
3. Indicative content: Of poor quality; unsatisfactory. He hates mirrors because they don't reflect him. Some students might suggest that the mirror reminds him that he is no longer human.
4. The word suggests a violent action.
5. Answers will vary.

## Knowledge and understanding

1. A few hours
2. Because he hadn't seen his reflection in the mirror
3. Dracula is attracted by the blood and is going to bite the narrator.
4. He throws it out of the window.

## Writing skills

1. Answers will vary but should include some of the following: threatening, shocking, frightening, unnerving, unsettling, tense.
2. I heard the sound of rain outside my window, which I normally find relaxing but on this occasion it made me feel nervous and I found I was unable to close my eyes so I sat up in bed and it was then I heard footsteps.
   Students may substitute some words to increase the effectiveness, such as adding an adjective before 'sound' – e.g. 'incessant' or substitute 'constant drumming'. Reward any attempts to use language to add atmosphere.

## Check your skills

Answers will vary. A good answer will build on Harker's 'vague unease' without going too far. Sentences will be varied and the writing will create tension. It will also contain effective descriptions of the interior of the castle. Weaker answers will not be able to maintain the unease and tension or may be confusing.

# Unit 3: An awesome stranger

*Pages 50–55*

## Word power

1. a. Gaped
   b. Scowl
   c. and d. Answers will vary.
2. Answers will vary but students should identify thunder with anger and violence.
3. The word 'crust' implies a rough or hardened layer. The jewels would have created a rough feel.
4. He was holding a sprig of holly which would have contrasted with his fearsome appearance. It might have seemed like a Christmas joke.
5. Answers will vary but a good answer will describe the creature and the effect it had on the onlookers. Weaker answers are likely to concentrate on the

creature, neglecting the impact on the people in the room. Strong answers will provide a detailed description linked to the effect each detail has on the narrator and the others in the room.

## Knowledge and understanding

1. His red eyes
2. The horse was a giant. It was green. It was also bad-tempered or angry.
3. The sword had been used to kill married men, making their wives into widows.
4. This shows us how frightening the Green Knight was. Even fierce dogs wouldn't attack him.
5. Answers will vary. Students may suggest that the knight's lack of normal war equipment made him more frightening because he seemed invincible, being aware that no-one would even attempt to fight him. He therefore didn't need a sword, shield or armour.

## Writing skills

1. a. Answers will vary. There are plenty of examples of alliteration. The technique emphasises certain words and phrases but it also provides the text with rhythm.
   b. Answers will vary.
2. Answers will vary. A good answer will link the description to the effect on the narrator and the reader.

## Check your skills

Answers will vary. A good answer will use many of the features of the original text, as directed in the bullet points. The dialogue should also fit the tone of the original, making the Knight sound fearsome and King Arthur using regal, formal language.

# Unit 4: Hidden

*Pages 56–61*

## Word power

1. a. Clear
   b. Distress
2. a. Damp and sticky
   c. He is extremely frightened
3. a. The smugglers are engaged in illegal activity so they would not want anyone to watch them or talk carelessly about their activities.

**b.** They are likely to be physically violent, possibly even killing anyone who threatened their activities. Smuggling was punished very severely in those days so the risks were great.

4. Answers will vary. Good answers will focus on the narrator's thoughts and feelings, building tension. Some students may include the return of the diary's owner, catching, or nearly catching the narrator prying. Weaker answers may focus on actions rather than thoughts and feelings.

## Knowledge and understanding

1. True statements: a. John was already quite tense when he heard the sound of the smugglers.
   d. John knew that smugglers have a violent reputation.
   e. John still remembers how he felt when he realised that he was trapped.
2. They would have thought he was a spy, or likely to betray them to the authorities. They would have reacted violently, possibly even killing him.
3. He climbed up between a coffin and the wall
4. Sample answer: A church vault would be ideal because it is hidden from view, rarely visited, in a place that would be unlikely to be raided by the authorities. Churches are not usually connected with illegal activities so no-one would suspect.

## Reading skills

1. The minute seemed longer than a normal minute because tension tends to make our experience of time slow down. Students should refer to 'that seemed as an age'.
2. Students are likely to choose curious and quick-thinking but opinions might differ about whether he's brave or foolhardy. Any answer supported by evidence is acceptable.
3. **a.** The ferret is being used to chase rabbits out of their burrows. They are then caught by the dog.
   **b.** John sees himself being hunted by the smugglers.
   **c.** Answers will vary but a good answer is likely to refer to the rabbit symbolising a helpless victim while the ferret is seen as vicious hunter ('eyes gleaming in the dark' – a powerful image of evil intent). The gun and lurcher represent certain capture and death. There is no possibility of escape.

## Check your skills

Answers will vary. Strong answers will refer to good examples of tension and suspense. These might include the following:

- The first sounds that alert him. He was already tense ('awful stillness' being broken). He doesn't know what is causing the noise.
- The sound approaches slowly. Tension built through the stretching of time (a minute that seemed like an age).
- Description of John's thoughts and feelings as the smugglers approach. The tension being ramped up through the image of the rabbit being hunted.
- The use of the voices getting closer and closer. John's realisation that they are smugglers and likely to be violent.
- The description of John's quick thinking leading to his hiding. Hitting his head on the roof because his actions are so panicked.
- In the final paragraph he is lying, waiting for the smugglers to arrive. He is 'breathing hard' – still very tense. Seeing the torchlight approach.

# Unit 5: Haunted by the past

*Pages 62–67*

## Word power

1. **a.** Solid
   **b.** Jump out threateningly
   **c.** Unimportant
2. Answers will vary but students should understand that the reader should feel a mixture of curiosity and fear.
3. **a.** 'A sudden chill' implying fear, you are being watched, that the house is trying to tell you something.
   **b.** It is haunted. Students may choose 'It is dangerous'. If so, encourage them to name the danger. The writer implies that the presence is supernatural rather than physical.
   **c.** Answers will vary.
4. Answers will vary. Reward answers that create an atmosphere of dread, using various senses.

## Knowledge and understanding

1. The blindfold implies total darkness
2. Sight
3.

| 1 | f. An owl hoots. |
|---|---|
| 2 | c. You come across something made of stone. |
| 3 | a. The moon comes out from behind a cloud. |
| 4 | g. You stand at a crossroads by a large statue. |
| 5 | h. You turn to look at the house. |
| 6 | b. A cloud covers the moon. |
| 7 | e. You run. |
| 8 | d. A child is sobbing. |

4. **a.** Answers will vary.
   **b.** Answers will vary.
5. Answers will vary but should include reference to the struggle between the man and boy and the expression on the man's face. Some students might notice that they are winged and connect the figures with Greek gods or mythology.

## Writing skills

1. Answers will vary but should refer to the way in which using the second person draws the reader into the scene.
2. Sample answer: Foxes are well-known for being alert, with strong senses of smell, sight and hearing. The fox is alert to any threat, so this also adds the inference that the garden is threatening.

3. Sample answer: The blank shutters are made to seem like the dead or blindfolded eyes of the house. Even so, the house speaks to you, just as a person might do. It's like being spoken to by a dead person or ghost.

## Check your skills

Answers will vary. A strong answer may also be written in the second person present tense but this isn't crucial. The most important quality is that this paragraph maintains the atmosphere of the original.

# Unit 6: Writing assessment

*Pages 68–69*

## Writing assessment

For writing assessment criteria, see pages 130-131.

# Unit 1: Understanding robots

*Pages 70–75*

## Word power

1. **a.** Sample answer: A robot is ideal for the job because no human lives need be put in danger.
   **b.** Answers will vary.
2. **a.** Answers will vary.
   **b.** Answers will vary.
3. **a.** Sample answer: … it might be contaminated.
   **b.** Sample answer: … the surrounding area was contaminated.
4. He sometimes forgot his lines.

## Knowledge and understanding

1. **a.** Repetitive and dangerous
   **b.** Sample answer: Nursing requires human qualities such as compassion so it would be unsuitable.
   Sample answer: Robots can only do what they're programmed for so they can't be creative.
2. Humans could never do those jobs because they are too dangerous or the environments are too hostile for them to survive in. Only robots could do them because they don't need food, water or air to continue working. Robots are stronger than humans and so can withstand extreme conditions (or similar).
3. Robots can't make decisions, they can only carry out pre-programmed actions so they could not manage people in the workplace.
4. Sample answer: The word 'learn' is in quotation marks to indicate that artificial intelligence allows robots to process more information but they can't really learn like humans. Robot learning isn't the same as human learning because robots can't understand the world like we can.

## Writing skills

1. Answers will vary but students should identify the main point in each paragraph.
2. Robot history
3. Answers will vary.

## Check your skills

Answers will vary. A strong answer will have well-chosen subheadings followed by relevant paragraphs. Each paragraph should have a topic sentence supported by evidence. Weaker answers are likely to include some irrelevant information so that paragraphs lack coherence.

# Unit 2: Learning about the past

*Pages 76–81*

## Word power

1. Women were not eligible to join the Geological Society of London until 1904.
2. Answers will vary.
3. Answers will vary.
4. **a.** Thirty inches of rain fell and the subsequent flooding made more than a thousand people homeless.
   **b.** The oil tanker struck the rocks in a storm but the subsequent oil spill poisoned very few seabirds.
5. Sample answer: Daniel's fear of heights as an adult was put down to the fact that he fell off a ladder as a child.

## Knowledge and understanding

1. This was when landslides exposed new fossils
2. To protect herself from falling rocks
3. Until then, many people did not believe that animals and plants could become extinct. Mary's discoveries of the remains of so many strange creatures never seen alive was convincing evidence that they had died out.
4. True statements are b and c.
5. A popular song was written about her in 1908. In 2010, 163 years after her death, the Royal Society included Anning in a list of the ten British women who have most influenced the history of science.
6. 'Fossil hunting didn't make Mary rich.'

## Reading skills

1. Sample answer: She was nearly killed. During a storm on 19 August 1800, 15-month-old Mary was being held in the arms of a neighbour, who was sheltering under a tree with two other women. Lightning struck the tree and all three women were killed.
2. Mary had a difficult childhood.
3. Answers will vary.
4. Answers will vary.

## Check your skills

Answers will vary. A strong answer will infer information from different parts of the text and bring it together to form a coherent view. Weaker answers may struggle to make inferences or include irrelevant information.

# Unit 3: Reporting the future

*Pages 82–87*

## Word power

1. **a.** a school lesson; having your hair cut
   **b.** These both require human skills that machines do not possess.
2. Sample answer: It uses a GPS signal to navigate and it also has some cameras to guide it around obstacles.
3. Our initial problem was how to make sure that the tent didn't collapse.
4. Answers will vary.
5. Answers will vary.

## Knowledge and understanding

1. It can deliver food in London. The robot courier is a six-wheel automated trolley. It can travel up to 4 miles per hour for roughly 10 miles. It uses a GPS signal. It has nine cameras to navigate and avoid obstacles.
2. 'land-based'. This implies that other sorts of robots (e.g. flying drones) have been used before.
3. To cope with the shortage of supply drivers when they are busy.
4. Having an accident; being picked on by passers-by; getting lost
5. Sample answer: The developers expected the public to react more strongly to the robots so they were surprised by the lack of reaction.

## Writing skills

1. Answers will vary.
2. **a.** Answers will vary but should include the idea that the quote makes the process seem simple. Students may also suggest that it makes the story livelier by adding a voice.
   **b.** The chief executive of Just Eat is a senior representative of a company that will be using the robots, so this adds credibility to the story.
3. Answers will vary.
4. Answers will vary.

## Check your skills

Answers will vary but a strong answer will incorporate most of the features of the model text. Weaker answers are likely to lack consistent tone or the right level of formality and may display more of the features of an advertisement or persuasive text.

# Unit 4: A modern marvel

*Pages 88–93*

## Word power

1. **a.** Answers will vary.
   **b.** Answers will vary.
2. **a.** Talking while the teacher is speaking to the class is considered rude.
   **b.** Opening the door for an old person is considered polite.
3. To get a job in France you need to have a good command of the language.
4. The sound was considered to be very clear.
5. Answers will vary but reward answers which include plenty of words and phrases from the original article.

## Knowledge and understanding

1. Speakers can communicate at great distances.
2. Telegraph, telephone, phonograph
3. This means that the voice heard from the record (a metal plate) sounds exactly like the person in real life.
4. This refers to recorded sound which can be posted around the world in the form of records.

## Reading skills

1. 'The discovery and successful working of the electric telegraph has familiarised us with achievements of science.'

2. **a.**

| Telegraph | Telephone | Phonograph |
|---|---|---|
| Messages can be transmitted across the world, read by skilled operators and printed. | Can clearly transmit the human voice and musical sounds, to any distance along wires. | Will enable a message of any length to be spoken onto a metal plate and sent by post to any part of the world, and the message will sound just like the original speaker. |

   **b.** Answers will vary.

3. **a.** The writer is obviously excited.
   **b.** The following words and phrases contribute to the tone: 'unlimited', 'unquestionably', 'most marvellous'.
   **c.** Answers will vary.

## Check your skills

Answers will vary. Strong answers will find plenty of examples of the writer's excitement and enthusiasm for new technology and will be able to explain how these words and phrases convey the writer's attitude. Weaker students may struggle to explain how the language conveys the writer's attitude.

# Unit 5: Reading assessment

*Pages 94–95*

## Reading assessment

1. Hell-raiser
2. Ada's mother thought these subjects would be less likely to make her life chaotic, like her father's. She thought sensible subjects like these would prevent her from becoming like her father (or similar).
3. Lovelace translated an essay on the Analytical Engine and her notes contained instructions on using the machine. These were the first program.
4. It could also be used to process music and letters
5. Answers will vary but should include the following points:
   - Her parents separated after a short marriage.
   - Her father was a famous poet who was regarded as mad, dangerous and immoral.
   - Lord Byron led a chaotic life.
   - Her mother was a mathematician and chose similar unconventional subjects for her daughter to study. Wanted her daughter to be more like herself than her ex-husband.
   - Her mother was very strict and insisted on Ada studying extremely hard. A pushy parent.
   Strong answers will draw out the contrasts between the two parents.
6. Answers will vary but should include the following points:
   - Girls didn't usually study maths and science.
   - Lovelace had to be educated at home because universities did not admit women.
   - Many mathematicians didn't believe that Ada could have written her notes because they didn't think that a woman was capable of the necessary advanced maths.
7. Answers should include the following points:
   - 'she could see the other applications of the machine.'
   - 'she understood that it computed symbols and so could also process music and letters.'
   - 'At the age of 12, Lovelace designed the plans of a steamdriven flying machine in the shape of a horse.'
8. Answers will vary. Strong answers will select information that is likely to appeal to young readers and express it in lively language using journalistic techniques learned during the chapter. They will also incorporate an understanding of why Ada Lovelace Day is celebrated and its relevance to today's young girls particularly. Weaker answers will be less lively and the information may not be fully integrated into the text.

# Student Book 1 Answers
## Chapter 4: Opinion and persuasion

## Unit 1: A call for change

*Pages 96–101*

### Word power

1. **a.** The number of animals dying is too large to count.
   **b.** I've told you countless times not to do that!
   The old church has stood on this site for countless years.
   There are countless good arguments against your stupid ideas.
2. **a.** Dying out
   **b.** Sample answer: The polar bear may become extinct.
3. It took all us morning to work out the best solution.
4. **a.** They must represent your views.
   **b.** Answers will vary but should include something like 'listen to others', 'express ideas clearly', 'understand your point of view and convey it rather than their own'.
5. Answers will vary.

### Knowledge and understanding

1. Generations to come, starving children, dying animals
2. The fish are now full of cancers.
3. She fears that the animals she would love to see will be extinct before her children can see them.
4. They are responsible adults whereas she is still a child.

### Writing skills

1.

| Question | Answer |
| --- | --- |
| What is going wrong in the world? | Animals are dying, becoming extinct, the ozone layer is damaged, air and water are polluted. |
| Who is to blame and why? | Adults who have allowed this to happen. |
| What should be done about it? | We should stop damaging the environment any further. |

2. Answers will vary but should refer to lists enabling her to emphasise the size of the problem and to draw attention to the variety of aspects of the natural world that are being destroyed. Lists also

enable her to create images in the minds of her audience so that the destruction seems more tragic.
3. **a.** An animal now extinct. The forests that once grew where there is now a desert
   **b.** Sample answer: These are images of destruction that are intended to make the audience feel sad, angry and guilty.
4. Sad, angry and guilty. References to the text will vary.

### Check your skills

Answers will vary. A strong answer will contain compelling descriptions of the effects of climate change using facts from the factfile. Weaker students may struggle to integrate the facts into persuasive sentences or may be limited in their use of rhetorical devices.

## Unit 2: Encouraging action

*Pages 102–107*

### Word power

1. **a.** By the time they reached the battle, the army was three thousand soldiers strong.
   **b.** Because one of our players was injured, the team was only ten players strong.
2. She uses it to compare life in Canada with the developing world (Brazil). The people of Canada have advantages denied to the people of the developing countries.
3. **b.** She means that if adults say something, then they should act on it.
4. Answers will vary.

### Knowledge and understanding

1. Sample answer: Just as a family thinks and works together, we are all (people and animals) affected by the damage to our environment so we should all act together to stop it.
2. **a.** Selfish
   **b.** Answers will vary.
3. Answers will vary but should comment on Canada's rich consumer lifestyle compared to Brazil's poverty.

**4.** Sample answer: This refers to the fact that it is simply a matter of luck if you are born rich in somewhere like Canada or poor in somewhere like Brazil. Poverty is a matter of chance.

**5.** All the money spent on war should be spent on finding environmental answers, ending poverty and finding global agreements.

**6.** Adults should show their love by improving the environment for their children and future generations.

## Reading skills

**1. a.** She is angry about the environmental damage done by adults and previous generations and their unwillingness to take action.

**b.** She sees the inequality in the world and the damage to the environment.

**c.** She fears what will happen if we don't do something about it urgently.

**2.** Sample answer: If I am only a child and I know this, why can't adults see the damage we are doing to our environment and take action?

**3. a.**

| Sadness | what you do makes me cry at night |
|---------|-----------------------------------|
| Desperation | please |

**b.** Answers will vary.

**c.** Answers will vary but should refer to the importance of ending the speech with an emotional plea so that the audience feels that it must respond by taking action.

## Check your skills

Answers will vary. A strong answer will be written clearly from the viewpoint of a young person, indicating why a young person might respond differently to an adult. Weaker students might respond to the content or the language of the speech but be less clear about the particular views of young people and why they might feel angry.

# Unit 3: Speaking from experience

*Pages 108–113*

## Word power

**1.** Sample answer: His experience was educational because he learned how disabled people are treated by the general public.

**2. a.** It suggests that shop staff were attracted to her because she looked glamorous and likely to buy their products.

**b.** Answers will vary.

**3.** Sarah was also treated badly in places other than shops. Explanations will vary.

**4. a.** She felt she wasn't accepted because she was using a wheelchair.

**b.** Answers will vary.

## Knowledge and understanding

**1.** 'for a while'

**2.** She seemed to disappear from view. She seemed to become invisible. She was ignored.

**3.** He means that she was ignored or treated as if she was unimportant. People didn't notice her.

**4.** They felt awkward and looked away.

**5.** Answers will vary.

## Writing skills

**1.**

| Para 1 | A |
|--------|---|
| 2 | B |
| 3 | B |
| 4 | B |
| 5 | C |
| 6 | C |
| 7 | C or B |
| 8 | D |
| 9 | D |

**2. a.**

| Para 1 | Present |
|--------|---------|
| 2 | Past |
| 3 | Present |
| 4 | Past |
| 5 | Past |
| 6 | Past |
| 7 | Past |
| 8 | Present |
| 9 | Present |

**b.** Sample answer: the present tense is used for two reasons: to describe the wife's normal life (which will continue after the operation) and to describe the current poor treatment of wheelchair users including a plea to change our behaviour.

**3.** Sample answer: The change in pronouns signals a change in purpose. The writer moves from describing particular experiences to talking about our everyday behaviour towards wheelchair users. The 'we' and 'you' are used persuasively to address society and the reader directly to encourage us to change our behaviour.

4. Sample answer: The phrase 'are still people' emphasises the fact that many people treat wheelchair users as if they are not human. The repetition of 'people' adds to the emphasis.

## Check your skills

Answers will vary. Strong answers will incorporate techniques and structure learned from the model text. Weaker answers may lack structure or persuasiveness.

# Unit 4: Support our campaign

*Pages 114–119*

## Word power

1. **a.** between or among
   **b.** Communicating, or similar
2. **a.** unorganised, free, improvised, made up, not organised by an adult
   **b.** Answers will vary.
3. tough and flexible
4. **a.** Answers will vary.
   **b.** Answers will vary.
5. If it gets too hot in the room, you can regulate the heating.
   The Football Association is an organisation that regulates football.

## Knowledge and understanding

1. Not involving parents, outside
2. Answers will vary.
3. Answers will vary but should refer to the need for children to deal with difficulties on their own, take responsibility for their actions, deal with adverse weather conditions or accidents without parental intervention. These experiences will enable them to gain confidence and cope with difficulties in the future, making them more resilient.
4. Answers will vary but should include the idea of children gradually becoming more physically daring (e.g. climbing trees or jumping over obstacles).
5. Answers will vary but should refer to the dangers of over-reacting, becoming violent or unstable.

## Reading skills

1. **a.** Sample answer: Adults reading the text probably played outside on their own when they were children so they will identify with the ideas of the text. It will prompt their own happy memories.
   **b.** Sample answer: They will remember their own happy childhood experiences and want the same positive experiences for their own children or the children of others.
2. **a.**

|  | Differences |
|---|---|
| Childhood of the past | Parents not involved; playing outside; made up physically active games; playing in gangs; interacting with other children and the environment. |
| Childhood of the present | Too much traffic, so playing indoors; plenty of indoor entertainment (e.g. computers, TV); parents worried about safety; parents don't have enough time to play; children often enrolled in organised clubs. |

   **b.** Answers will vary but should refer to the fact that play of the past is described positively, conjuring up a picture of a free, happy and healthy childhood whereas today's childhoods seems boring and restricted.
3. Discover and act on their own interests, ideas and passions.
   - Discover – makes children seem like explorers, making discoveries.
   - Act – makes the children sound confident and decisive.
   - Own – their own ideas, not what their parents choose for them.
   - Ideas – independent creativity – these are their ideas, not their parents'.
   - Passions – emotional – indicating a fulfilling life.

## Check your skills

Answers will vary. A strong answer will bring together all the ideas explored in the Reading skills section, supported by quotations from the text. Weaker students may repeat the statement from the task without providing enough textual reference to support it.

# Unit 5: Writing assessment

*Pages 120–121*

## Writing assessment

For writing assessment criteria, see pages 130-131.

## Unit 1: Adrenaline rush

*Pages 122–127*

### Word power

1. Answers will vary.
2. Intensifies. Explanations will vary.
3. Because you are travelling so fast that this seems like a short distance
4. Sample answer: The word is used to describe a sort of battle between forces. At this point, gravity is in control again.
5. Answers will vary but students should refer to a harmony between the skydiver and the air. As if he or she belongs in this environment.
6. Answers will vary. A strong answer will use language in a similar way to describe the stages of the dive. Weaker students are likely to struggle with vocabulary or clarity.

### Knowledge and understanding

1. The equipment weighs heavily on your back, the floor presses against your feet, and the straps pull on your legs and shoulders.
2. The wind
3. **D.** You jump from the plane.
   **E.** You are free falling.
   **A.** You pull the cord to open the parachute.
   **C.** Your parachute slows your descent.
   **B.** You land safely on the ground.
4. You feel victorious because you have defied gravity. Explanations why may vary.

### Writing skills

1. Sample answer: This makes it feel as if it is happening now; the writer is describing events as they are happening so you feel as if you are sharing the experience.
2. Soaring through the sky; 'only one mile left to fall'
3.

| The skydiver feels an adrenaline rush. In control. Thrilled. Excited |
| Rushing, then peaceful, calm |

4. Sample answer: 10 seconds in paragraph 1 – feeling supported by the wind. 60 seconds in paragraph 2 – you feel free. 5 seconds in

paragraph 3 – feels like a short time because you are hurtling towards the ground. You realise how many sensations are crammed into such a short time; how intense the experience is.

### Check your skills

Answers will vary. A strong answer will describe the astronaut's different feelings and sensations at each stage. Weaker students may struggle to differentiate between each stage or may rely too much on physical description.

## Unit 2: When the soldiers came

*Pages 128–133*

### Word power

1. Sample answer: This makes them seem more like machines or robots than human beings.
2. Firmly
3. **a.** Sample answer: the more junior soldiers, the lower ranked soldiers
4. Sample answer: 'heavy footsteps on the stairs' – the soldiers are described as being heavy and clumsy, the noise representing the violence of their actions. 'A window was banged shut' – this may have been caused by the wind but it represents the destruction of a community, an end.

### Knowledge and understanding

1. They were wearing steel helmets and green uniforms.
2. Sample answer: They were acting on an order.
3. Sample answer: This is likely to mean that people felt safe enough to leave their doors open. Not worried about burglars. A close community.
4. **a.** Answers will vary.
   **b.** Answers will vary.
5. Answers will vary but they should include references to the fact that they feared that they were being taken away for some time or possibly forever and that they were not going to be treated well.

## Reading skills

1. Quick-witted, confident
2.

| Bolt upright | Adds to the impression of them being like robots, inhuman. The word bolt is hard and metallic, like the soldiers. |
|---|---|
| Like tin soldiers in a toy car | A metallic, inhuman image but there's also a sort of grim humour. The soldiers are slightly comical. |

3. Answers will vary but students should show that they've understood her fear during this conversation. She will be hoping that she'll be let go and is looking for any sign of the decision that the officer has made.

## Check your skills

1. Answers will vary but should include some of the following:
   - Treading on the paper represents the soldiers' violence and disregard for human life. A metaphor for the destruction.
   - The helmet makes him seem to have a steel forehead, as if he has no brain, only steel. Like a machine, he cannot think for himself. A robot, not a human being.
2. Answers will vary but students should recognise that she comes across as intelligent, quick-witted and confident. She is also imaginative and perceptive in her description of details. Strong answers will support these points with relevant quotations and textual references.

# Unit 3: Confrontation

*Pages 134–139*

## Word power

1. **a.** moving slowly, heavily and awkwardly – lumbering moving quickly and easily, like a gymnast – agility
   **b.** We might find the agility surprising because bears are so big and heavy.
2. He assumed that bears were slow and lumbering.
3. Sample answer: The bear was charging at him but then 'he veered sideways and disappeared into the scrub'. He is relieved that the bear has decided to run off rather than attack him. He feels that the bear is no longer a threat. He is still feeling the physical effects of his fear, making him 'light-headed' – dizzy.

4. Answers will vary. A strong answer will use the techniques from the model text to describe the encounter. The piece may become humorous, using the bear as a simile for the deputy head teacher. Weaker students may struggle to describe the encounter in detail and rush to a conclusion before building tension.

## Knowledge and understanding

1. **a.** He felt relieved because he thought the bear was moving away from him.
   **b.** He then realised that the bear was moving around in order to attack him from another direction.
2. He was shivering because he was frightened but also because he had been bathing in a cold river.
3. Students should identify the following facts:
   - Bears have a strong sense of smell.
   - They are huge and powerful.
   - They have poor eyesight.
   - They can move quickly and with agility.
   - They can run at 35 mph.
4. He began shouting, making as much noise as possible in an attempt to scare him off.
5. Answers should include the following:
   - Stay downwind of it so that it can't smell you.
   - Don't try to outrun it because they are very fast.
   - Back away gently so as not to attract attention.
   - If the bear attacks, then fight back.
   - Try making a noise because that might scare it off.

## Writing skills

1. Answers will vary.
2. Answers will vary but should refer to the way that dashes work to pace the writing, so that the writer can insert short gaps for effect and emphasis.
3. **a.** 'Neither of us moved. For minutes. Three, maybe four – it seemed like hours. [both] And then, with a snort, he turned slowly round and lumbered back into the bush. [the bear] I felt like the most fortunate man alive.' [Grieve]
   **b.** Sample answer: The short sentence 'Neither of us moved' emphasises the way that they both froze and the 'for minutes' gives the reader an idea of how long they remained motionless. The short sentence, followed by the non-sentence, is punctuated with a full stop to stop the flow of the narrative abruptly.

## Check your skills

Answers will vary. Strong answers will use the sentence structures explored in the previous section to create tension and excitement through speeding up and slowing the pace. Weaker students may struggle to control the punctuation for effect.

# Unit 4: Advice for Victorian women

*Pages 140–145*

## Word power

1. Starting with advice on accidents might make the reader think that an accident is likely to happen.
2. **a.** Accidents are likely to happen.
   **b.** All the old teacher could think about was her impending retirement.
   His impending exams kept him awake at night.
   We all wished him luck for his impending operation.
3. Answers will vary.
4. A woman who tries to help a man is likely to get in the way and therefore prevent him from dealing with the problem.
5. Provide extra parking spaces for the increased number of cars; employ more stewards to deal with the extra people

## Knowledge and understanding

1. Because accidents are likely to happen and so it is better to be prepared for them
2. Travelling has become less dangerous because of modern invention and skill (technology).
3. Keep still and be ready for action.
4. **a.** If a man is in charge then let him get on with it and don't get in the way.
   **b.** If no man is present, then she will have to deal with it, but she should do nothing until she is forced to act.
5. Sample answer: If you expect accidents to happen at any moment, then you'll spoil the pleasure of travelling because you'll always be on edge.
6. Statement **b**

## Reading skills

1. **a.** Sample answer:

| coolness and self-possession in the time of danger are not only the greatest safeguards against impending accident, but the best life-preservers | being calm when you're in danger is the best way of preventing accidents and it is also likely to save your life |
|---|---|
| that accident has become an established fact | that accident actually happens |

   **b.** Sample answer: First of all, it's a rule that being calm when you're in danger is the best way of preventing accidents and it is also likely to save your life when that accident actually happens.
2. Sample answer:
   • 'courage and calmness' are modern female qualities
   • 'the weaker' sex
   • 'If there is no man, the woman will have to act for herself'
   • 'feminine physical weakness'
   These words and phrases create the impression that, although women were seen as weaker than men and that men should naturally be in charge, women were perfectly capable of being brave and calm.

## Check your skills

1. Answers will vary but students should see that the expectation is that men will naturally want to protect women and will not want them to get in the way.
2. Sample answer: If you are constantly worrying about accidents, you will not enjoy travelling so you might as well stay at home, making sure that no accidents happen to you there. She is poking fun at women who are obsessed with the dangers of travelling and are over-cautious.
3. Answers will vary.

# Unit 5: Reading assessment

*Pages 146–147*

## Reading assessment

1. True statements: b, d and e
2. Answers will vary. Students should explain that O'Farrell is feeling angry at her own foolishness and guilty. Strong answers will include comments on some of the following:
   - Repetition of 'He can't swim' to express her guilt and the way that her thoughts go 'round and round'. It's like a voice in her head.
   - 'He can't swim.' as a short sentence for emphasis and to shock.
   - Use of 'I've brought him out' to express guilt – that it's her fault if her son drowns.
   - Repetitive pattern reflects the way that her thoughts revolve and her swimming action.
   - 'Deep sea' to express danger.
   - Anger expressed through calling her advisor 'someone' and 'an idiot'.
   - From the second sentence onwards, each sentence is a repetition, adding more information each time. This is O'Farrell's way of punishing herself by reminding herself of her own stupidity.

   Weaker answers may comment on her feelings of anger and guilt but may not support views with evidence.

3. Answers will vary. Strong answers will comment on some of the following:
   - Present tense conveys immediacy.
   - Strong physical verbs (kick, stretch etc.) convey violent physical effort.
   - Commas used to slow down the action to create tension (I kick again, stretch, and this time I reach it).
   - Short sentence, 'I miss.' is used to convey shock and disappointment.
   - Repetition of 'I' re-enforces the tension that O'Farrell feels because she is responsible for the situation and she is the only one who can save her son.

4. Answers will vary but strong answers should include some of the following:
   - She obviously cares about her son because she doesn't let him know they're in danger so that he won't be frightened.
   - She regrets her impulsive action and wishes she had been more sensible but she's a natural risk-taker.
   - She enjoys a little danger, which might make her more fun as a parent.
   - She wants her son to have exciting experiences.

   These should all be supported by references to the text or direct quotation.

   Some students may disagree with the statement and judge that she was too impulsive to be regarded as a good mother. This view should also be rewarded if it is supported by references to the text.

# Student Book 1 Answers
## Chapter 6: Arguments and essays

## Unit 1: Freedom and captivity

*Pages 148–153*

### Word power

1. The stripes make the tiger stand out from its surroundings. Some students might understand that, in its natural habitat, the stripes would blend in, camouflaging and protecting the tiger so this makes the animal seem out of place in the zoo.
2. It would lurk in order to hunt
3. Sample answer: Scientists watched the tigers carefully to learn how they behave in the wild. Observing is to watch carefully and take note of what you see.  Seeing and watching in the other examples are too passive.
4. Sample answer: The article makes the point that interacting with a real live animal is more likely to make you appreciate it because you get a better sense of it being alive and moving, unlike TV pictures or stuffed animals. It makes more of an impression on your senses. The experience is likely to be more intense and memorable.
5. Sample answer: Keeping alive. Zoos keep some endangered animals alive and try to breed them so that they can be reintroduced to the wild.
6. Sample answer: My brother is a very good DJ, so he is in demand at parties.
   You should train to be a computer programmer because they are very much in demand these days.

### Knowledge and understanding

1. We know it is small because the poet tells us that the tiger stalks 'The few steps of his cage'.
2. Sample answer: These stanzas describe what the tiger would be doing in the wild. The poet thinks that he shouldn't be in a zoo and therefore that he should be doing these things.
3. Answers will vary but evidence to support the view that the poet dislikes zoos should include some of the following:
   - The cage is small.
   - The tiger is stressed or made angry by being in a zoo.
   - The tiger is out of place and can't act naturally.
   - The tiger is locked up like a prisoner.

- In the final stanza he seems to be longing for freedom.

4. 1 – d, 2 – b, 3 – a, 4 – e, 5 – c. Students may suggest points 4 and 5 should be reversed, as the content is quite similar.

### Writing skills

1.

| What the tiger should be doing | What the tiger is doing |
|---|---|
| lurking | stalks |
| sliding | ignoring |
| snarling | Is locked |
| Baring his fangs | Stalking |
| Terrorising | hears |
|  | stares |

**a. and b.** Answers will vary but should link these ideas together to create the two contrasting impressions.
2. Answers will vary.

### Check your skills

Answers will vary. A strong answer will blend the ideas from the poem and the techniques from the article. Weaker students may struggle to write the anti-zoo sentiments of the poem in the form of a prose argument.

## Unit 2: Reptile alert

*Pages 154–159*

### Word power

1. He was going to buy a 'replacement' snake but the other tenants protested, so he didn't.
2. **a.** They are frightened of them
   **b.** Answers will vary.
3. Sample answer: Buying small animals to feed to snakes supports the industry that supplies snakes and which the writer would like to see banned because it is cruel.
4. Sample answer: They should be free and wild, 'exploring lush jungles and swamps and experiencing all the sensory pleasures that they're designed to enjoy'.

5. Figurative language such as 'sky-high' makes the statement sound more dramatic.

## Knowledge and understanding

1. Because his pet snake had escaped and he was looking for it
2. This implies that she was worried that the snake might attack her during the night.
3. The neighbours complained, and either he listened or his landlord prevented him buying another.
4. • Snakes need special lighting and food.
   • Snakes shun contact with humans.
   • Being held, touched, petted or passed around is stressful and leaves snakes prone to illness and injury.
   • Snakes eat rabbits, mice and crickets.
5. Answers will vary.
6. At least 75 percent of pet snakes die within one year in a human home.

## Reading skills

1. Answers will vary but should refer to some of these points: the desire to draw her readers into the article through a story; linking her views to personal experiences makes them more understandable; the anecdote provides an example which supports her views.
2. **a.** She is making the point that snakes can never really be pets like cats or dogs.
   **b.** 'replacement'. This makes the point that the neighbour was treating a living animal as if it was an object or a possession which could be easily replaced.
3. Answers will vary but students should point out examples of effective language choices such as 'killing', 'cruel', 'mortality' which attract the reader's attention and create the impression of a cruel and abusive business only interested in profit with no concern for animal welfare. Students may also comment on the use of direct statements 'It's a dirty business' and 'Captivity is cruel' which sound confident and shocking.
4. **a.** Answers will vary, but points similar to these:

| How wild snakes live | How pet snakes live |
| --- | --- |
| Free to explore their proper environment, enjoying their natural habitat | Imprisoned in aquariums that are too small for them |

**b.** Answers will vary. Strong answers will comment on the use of descriptive language (verbs and noun phrases) to make the contrast as dramatic and persuasive as possible. We are encouraged to see the differences from a snake's point of view, share in their experiences.

## Check your skills

Answers will vary but students should comment on some of the following:

- The shocking effect of the metaphorical subheading (explored earlier in the unit).
- Evidence provided in the form of statistics to make the argument convincing.
- Use of 'It is believed that…' (passive voice) to sound formal and academic.
- Use of ironic quotation marks ('Must-have pets').
- Image of 'dark basements or garages' to paint a sordid picture.
- 'tossed outside like trash' – violent image (alliteration and simile).

# Unit 3: Animal superstar

*Pages 160–165*

## Word power

1. Scott bestowed the affections of a mother on Jumbo. Bestowed motherly love on him.
2. Sample answer: They were moving slowly, in a stately way, like a royal procession.
3. **a.** Sample answer: Yesterday, I was engaged doing my homework when my phone rang.
   **b.** Answers will vary.
4. **a.** Slowly and carefully
   **b.** Answers will vary.
5. His mother's control

## Knowledge and understanding

1. Looked after him like a parent would have.
2. Sample answer: Jumbo is described as a baby and as 'my boy'. Describes himself as being like a mother and father to a child (loving him like a child). Sharing experiences with Jumbo as a parent would with a child. Scot clearly loved Jumbo.
3. Sample answer: '… but for once he did not obey the order' implies that this is an exception and that he usually obeyed orders.
4. Sample answer: Scott isn't worried because Jumbo walks slowly and always looks where he is

going, so he was bound to spot the child and avoid him (supported by relevant quotations).

5. Students may feel the mother's rough handling of the child suggests she is angry and may tell the child off or punish it. She is clearly distraught (screaming), however, her reaction is more distress than anger – and the snatching up of the child was a maternal reaction to the peril she thought it was in: her natural instinct was to remove the child quickly. She may then tell the child off, but most likely she will keep a closer eye on her child to make sure it doesn't run away again.

## Writing skills

1. Answers will vary.
2. **a.** Sample answer: Jumbo is described as gentle and caring, making sure he doesn't hurt the child. He is calm and in control.
   **b.** Sample answer: The mother is distraught and frantic. She screams and picks her child up roughly. She is out of control.
   **c.** Answers will vary.

## Check your skills

Answers will vary. Strong answers will incorporate information from the text and will use some of the techniques typical of 19th century writers effectively. Weaker students may find the formality of the language difficult to sustain; however, any attempt to construct long sentences or archaic vocabulary should be rewarded.

# Unit 4: An old warrior

*Pages 166–171*

## Word power

1. **a.** They are watching for poachers
   **b.** Answers will vary.
2. A mountain peak and a tree. Reasons will vary.
3. **a.** This implies that he knows that he is the last of his kind and is sad.
   **b.** Answers will vary.
4. 'The fate' refers to what will happen to a specific thing or person whereas 'fate' is an abstract concept like truth or duty.
   **a.** She decided that it was fate that made her choose that road on that day.
   **b.** He was worried about the fate of all those poor starving animals.

## Knowledge and understanding

1. He is becoming too old
2. Five
3. They kill rhinos and hack off their horns to sell them on the Asian medicine market.
4. Answers will vary but students should identify the overall pessimistic tone of the article, supported by evidence (e.g. 'a slim chance', 'his appetite for struggle fading').

## Reading skills

1. Students should pick 'sad' and 'guilty'. Stronger students should be able to explain why a reader might feel guilty.
2. Sample answer: This question sets up the whole article because the rest of the article is the writer's way of answering it. It puts the reader in the writer's position by asking us to think about this question.
3. **a.** Answers will vary but should include the idea that the soldiers are guarding something precious and that they care about Sudan and what happens to him. That humans do care about animals threatened by extinction.
   **b.** Answers will vary but should include the idea that it's really an image of brutality because it shows us what humans have done to rhinos and how endangered they are. It's human brutality which has caused this disaster. If it wasn't for human brutality, Sudan would not need soldiers to guard him.
4. Jones is using the sky to represent the threat to Sudan.
5. Sample answer: Comparing Sudan to an old warrior implies that he had struggled hard to survive but is now too old to keep fighting. Students may also refer to how a rhino looks (armoured like a warrior) so that the image works physically too.

## Check your skills

Answers will vary but students should comment on:

- images of sadness – e.g. 'His eye is a sad black dot in his massive wrinkled face'
- images of strength – e.g 'His head is a marvellous thing… a majestic rectangle of strong bone and leathery flesh – a head that expresses pure strength'
- how the writer contrasts the images of Sudan's strength with the fact that he is really vulnerable (e.g. 'such a mighty head can in reality be so vulnerable').

**117**

# Unit 5: Writing assessment

*Pages 172–173*

## Writing assessment

For writing assessment criteria, see pages 130-131.

# Chapter 1: Characters and setting

## Unit 1: First impressions

*Pages 4–5*

### Activity 1: Word power

Students may have selected any of the adjectives that describe Gollum and his surroundings. Weak answers are likely to be brief and focus on giving a synonym or simple explanation of the word chosen. Stronger answers will unpack the connotations of the chosen word in order to explain how it contributes to the picture of Gollum.

### Activity 2: Knowledge and understanding

Answers will vary, as it depends on student perception. Look for engagement with the range of authorial intentions.

### Activity 3: Reading skills

Answers will vary, as some words are interchangeable. Sample answer:

I think Tolkien is trying to make Gollum seem **gruesome**. An **effective** way he does this is by creating a **dismal** setting. Phrases like 'deep down here' and 'roots of the mountain' make a picture of a **gloomy** place. Another **important** technique which helps to **repel** the reader is the description of Gollum's physical features, including his 'slimy' skin and paddle feet, which make him seem quite **inhuman**. Tolkien also uses vocabulary like 'prowling' and 'lurking' that makes Gollum seem **threatening**.

### Check your skills

Answers will vary.

## Unit 2: Flashback

*Pages 6–7*

### Activity 1: Knowledge and understanding

| Past tense (A) | | Present tense (B) | |
|---|---|---|---|
| 'They didn't' | 'I was plump' | 'It's alright' | 'I'm worrying' |
| 'I arrived' | 'They brought' | 'Nobody drives' | 'I press' |
| | | 'He says' | 'I remind' |

### Activity 2: Knowledge and understanding

Sample answers have been provided as a guide.

| Clue from the text | Possible inferences |
|---|---|
| 'But it's alright.' | The narrator is trying to reassure himself. He seems quite brave. |
| 'that narrow rocky road from the village' | The narrator knows he has been taken somewhere far away. Deep down, he may realise that it's a difficult place to get to and his parents are unlikely to come. |

### Activity 3: Writing skills

Answers will vary. Stronger answers will include sensory writing and a range of sentence lengths. Weaker answers will vary little from the original response provided.

### Check your skills

Annotations should be as follows:

- Present tense at the beginning to show we are in the here and now: 'The bag rattles'.
- Shift to past tense when the memory begins: 'I loved that truck'.
- Sights and sounds to make the memory vivid: 'red, green and blue', 'brum, brum, brum'.
- Short sentence emphasises emotion: 'I loved that truck'.
- Too many adjectives in a list here – pick the most important: 'old, battered, tiny, silver truck'.

## Unit 3: Under the surface

*Pages 8–9*

### Activity 1: Knowledge and understanding

The poet describes the quiet, empty station (2). The poet lists the plants and nature he can see from the train window (3). The poet explains that he can see and hear birds (4). The poet is remembering a day when his train stopped unexpectedly (1).

## Activity 2: Reading skills

**a.** All of the themes listed are arguably explored and therefore could be ticked.

**b.** Weaker answers will indicate limited understanding of the way themes are represented in the poem. Stronger answers will show insight into the relationship between themes through well-chosen quotations.

**c.** Answers will vary, but in broad terms students should agree with statement A and disagree with statement B. Weaker answers are likely to feature limited explanation. Stronger answers will offer deeper explanation justified by further reference to the text.

## Check your skills

Answers will vary, as dependent on self-assessment.

# Unit 4: Imprisoned in the past

*Pages 10–11*

## Activity 1: Knowledge and understanding

a. – Accurate but misses the key points.

b. – Accurate and includes all key information.

c. – Accurate but includes an unnecessary detail.

## Activity 2: Reading skills

**a.** Sample answers have been suggested below.

| Clue | What I can infer |
|---|---|
| 'I'll cut your throat!' | The man has a knife and is willing to use it. He's used to violence. |
| 'all in coarse gray' | The man's clothing is poor and dull, and may be some sort of uniform. |
| 'with a great iron on his leg' | The man won't be able to walk freely. He has recently been a prisoner. |
| 'an old rag tied round his head' | The man has been trying to hide, or is cold, or has an injury. |
| 'A man who had been soaked in water, and smothered in mud, and lamed by stones' | The man has been on a long and difficult journey. |
| 'teeth chattered in his head as he seized me by the chin' | The man is cold. |

**b.** Answers may vary but most likely inferences are:

- Dickens wants to increase the drama. – 3
- The man is really a ghost. – 1
- The man has been hiding amongst the graves. – 2

## Check your skills

Sample answers have been suggested below.

| Clues about the character Mrs Gargery, Pip's older sister | What might be inferred |
|---|---|
| Pip says she has 'a hard and heavy hand'. | She is very strict and often hits Pip. |
| She 'almost always wears a coarse apron'. | She works hard and doesn't have time to care about her appearance. |
| Pip is 'never allowed a candle' at night. | She is keen to save money, or she is unkind. |

# Unit 5: A test of character

*Pages 12–13*

## Activity 1: Reading skills

Answers a, c and e are all incorrect as they miss the key point of the passage. Answers b and d both have merit but the best answer is **b**.

## Activity 2: Knowledge and understanding

**a.**
1. Something else
2. Murdina Galloway
3. A mainlander
4. A niece of Mrs Farriss
5. She

**b.** Answers may vary but may include the following:

Murdina is dark-haired, dark-eyed and pale.
Murdina looks very different to the Hirta women.
Murdina's eyes are not creased but huge and round.
Murdina's hands are not roughened by work.

## Activity 3: Reading skills

Answers may vary, but a good answer will include the following:

- Words and phrases from the text ('something else', 'smooth and pale and long-fingered) and what these suggest (e.g. how Quill is drawn to Murdina's difference, Quill's detailed attention to her).
- A comment about the five different references to Murdina in the first paragraph and how this suggests that he pays her immediate and strong attention.
- Reference to the comparisons in the text ('Christ himself', 'peat-dark' eyes) and that these suggest he sees her as a miracle and how closely he looks at her.

## Check your skills

Answers will vary but should include at least two reasons, and may focus on:

- quality of spelling
- accuracy about the text
- use of informal language
- depth of explanation.

# Chapter 2: Action and atmosphere

## Unit 1: A dramatic opening

*Pages 14–15*

### Activity 1: Word power

| The target word is... | Which is being used as an... (adverb or adjective)? | To describe... |
|---|---|---|
| roughly | adverb | The action of *shaking* |
| properly | adverb | The way he can see his mum |
| slightly | adverb | How her face is lit up |
| mouthed | adjective | Mum's warnings |
| sudden | adjective | His mother putting a hand over his mouth |
| questioning | adjective | A frown |

### Activity 2: Writing skills

Answers will vary but students are likely to agree with the second and fourth statement and disagree with the third and fifth statement. Weak explanations will lack detail. Stronger explanations will show detailed understanding of the text.

## Check your skills

Answers will vary but should address the given success criteria, including:

- a synonym or rephrasing of breathing
- strong language choice to show panic
- detail to show the storyteller's feelings.

## Unit 2: An unusual companion

*Pages 16–17*

### Activity 1: Word power

Answers will vary but pupil's word choices may include: nursery, fireplace, rocking chair, runners, chimney breast.

### Activity 2: Writing skills

a. Answers may vary. Examples for each have been provided.

   A long sentence full of detail about place and actions: *There was the chimney breast and fireplace, there was the window closed and bolted and with two wooden bars across it, such as all nurseries have to guard the children from falling out; there was no other door.*

   A short sentence which shows the narrator's confusion: *The room had been empty.*

b. Answers may vary. Weaker answers may depend on spooky cliché and are unlikely to adopt the tone and features of the original. Stronger answers will maintain the narrator's voice and the pace and tone of the action.

## Check your skills

Answers will vary. Some pupils may not be able to identify the given features in their own writing, not be able to edit for improvement. Stronger answers will include the listed features or show an ability to edit for improvement at the second stage.

## Unit 3: An awesome stranger

*Pages 18–19*

### Activity 1: Knowledge and understanding

a. Students may select words such as: openly, honest, hero, nobility, grace.

b. Students may select phrases such as: 'opening his heart honestly', 'your ally and your good friend', 'come here to destroy him'.

### Activity 2: Reading skills

Students should tick: a, d, e and g.

### Activity 3: Writing skills

Answers will vary. Weaker answers will lack detail and describe the face as a whole. Stronger answers are likely to include greater detail and references to a range of facial features, with alliteration used to draw attention to at least one feature.

## Check your skills

Answers will vary as dependent on self-assessment.

# Unit 4: Hidden

*Pages 20–21*

### Activity 1: Word power

Students are likely to choose words such as: slithered, curled, crawled, swallowing.

### Activity 2: Knowledge and understanding

- The showman bangs on the door again. 4
- The showman reveals what he wants. 6
- Fog rises from the river to cover the city. 2
- Someone speaks to the showman. 5
- We are told it is night. 1
- The showman bangs on a door. 3

### Activity 3: Reading skills

Students should select either answer 2 or 3 and their choice will dictate what they go on to say about the author's intent. Stronger answers will explain the link between the author's choice and the effect on the reader.

### Check your skills

Answers will vary. Weaker answers and explanations will show little awareness of how a reader can be manipulated by sequencing action. Stronger answers will reveal insight into how story-telling plays with sequence in order to maximise impact on the reader.

# Unit 5: Haunted by the past

*Pages 22–23*

### Activity 1: Word power

'Listen'; 'Reach up and still the starships'; 'Look at your fingers'

### Activity 2: Reading skills

Student responses will vary but likely answers have been indicated below:

| Implied meaning | Relevant clue from the text |
| --- | --- |
| When he was younger, the boy may have been interested in geography. | 'The comforter is a golden map of the world' |

| The boy liked reading. | 'A place to curl up with a comic book' |
| --- | --- |
| The boy's parents bought him lots of toys. | 'A Lego skyscraper sits on a low table. Action figures patrol a nearby shelf' |
| The boy had a lot of plans for when he was an adult. | 'a house the boy drew when he was not even nine' |
| Someone may be breaking in. | 'the splintering of wood' |
| No one has been in the room for a long time. | 'black with dust' |

### Activity 3: Writing skills

Students' writing will vary but should include imperative verbs, description of a range of objects, clues for the reader.

### Check your skills

Answers will vary, dependent on self-assessment

# Chapter 3: Explanations and insights

## Unit 1: Understanding robots

*Pages 24–25*

### Activity 1: Knowledge and understanding

True statements are:

- The text explains what nanobots are.
- The text gives examples of what nanobots might be used for.
- The text informs us about how nanobots are currently used in medicine.
- The text asks us to imagine a future in which nanobots are used in different ways.

### Activity 2: Writing skills

**a.** Information for paragraph 1: 1, 4 and 6
Information for paragraph 2: 2, 3 and 5
**b.** Answers will vary.
**c.** Furthermore and similarly

### Check your skills

Answers will vary but stronger answers will include:

- a topic sentence
- connecting adverbials, correctly used.

# Unit 2: Learning about the past

*Pages 26–27*

## Activity 1: Word power

husbandman – farmer; verily – certainly; prithee – please; damsel – young unmarried woman; apothecary – chemist.

## Activity 2: Knowledge and understanding

a. Robert
b. He was a potter – someone who made plates and bowls.
c. 'patient building up'
d. 'a new epoch'

## Activity 3: Reading skills

1809–1882; 1825; 1831; 1840.

## Check your skills

Sample answer

1825 Darwin moved to Edinburgh to study medicine
1831 Darwin graduated from university
1840 Darwin published *Zoology of the Voyage of the Beagle.*
1882 Darwin died.

# Unit 3: Reporting the future

*Pages 28–29*

## Activity 1: Knowledge and understanding

a. Statements 1, 3, 4 and 5 should all be ticked. Only the fact of the robot being built at London University does not date the article.
b. Answers will vary.

## Activity 2: Writing skills

| Examples | Imperative | Modal verb | Repetition |
|---|---|---|---|
| Drones cause danger… | NO | YES | YES |
| Will humans move to other planets… | YES | YES | YES |

## Check your skills

Sample answer

| Headline | Opening sentence | Attention-grabbing techniques |
|---|---|---|
| Clone your dog and never have to say goodbye | Don't worry about losing your much-loved pet – scientists are suggesting that we will soon be able to clone our dogs and keep them with us forever. | Imperative (don't worry) Repetition ('clone') Modal verb ('will') |
| A trip into space – the best present ever | If you're an adventurous person, you might be glad to hear that a trip to space could be on your wish list soon. | Repetition ('trip to space') Modal verb ('might') |

# Unit 4: A modern marvel

*Pages 30–31*

## Activity 1: Word power

a. At peak times – 'During the busy hours of the day'
b. At the Mansion House stop – 'At the Mansion House Terminus'
c. The tunnels are 65 feet deep – 'the tunnels run to a depth of sixty-five feet'
d. Passengers will use a ramp – 'passengers will walk down a gentle incline'

## Activity 2: Reading skills

| Passive | Active |
|---|---|
| The books were given out (by the teacher). | The teacher gave out the books. |
| The evidence was examined (by the police). | The police examined the evidence. |
| The dog's ball was thrown (by me). | I threw the dog's ball. |
| A goal was scored (by the footballer). | The footballer scored a goal. |

## Check your skills

In 2013, the Mayor of London **officially opened** The Shard. Originally, **people knew** the building as London Bridge Tower but **they renamed it** after **some critics described it** as 'a shard of glass'. **Renzo Piano designed** The Shard in 2000. The **church spires across the city of London inspired** him.

# Chapter 4: Opinion and persuasion

## Unit 1: A call for change

*Pages 32–33*

### Activity 1: Word power

| To show difficulty | To encourage and persuade |
|---|---|
| hard | build a better world |
| inaction and denial | good news |
| persevere | our children |
| urgency of the challenge | unleash the creative power |
| work tirelessly | |

### Activity 2: Writing skills

Sample answer

| Technique | Example |
|---|---|
| Emotive language | 'a world that is safer, cleaner, and healthier than the one we found; and a future that is worthy of our children' |
| List of three | Three sentences beginning 'we know' in the first paragraph |
| Inclusive pronouns | 'we don't have much time left' |

### Check your skills

Answers will vary. Weaker answers may focus on only one or two techniques. Stronger answers will refer to more techniques and give examples.

## Unit 2: Encouraging action

*Pages 34–35*

### Activity 1: Knowledge and understanding

Link 2 – A, 3 – D, 4 – C, 5 – H, 6 – E, 7 – G , 8 – F

### Activity 2: Reading skills

| Technique | Example | Analysis of effect |
|---|---|---|
| A strong rhythm | **Answer:** any of the Shakespearean lines | Nearly all the lines have 10 syllables in a *de-dum, de-dum, de-dum, de-dum, de-dum* pattern, which gives the speech a powerful pattern of beats. |

| Contrast | **Answer:** 'fair nature' / 'hard-favour'd rage' | Comparing the men's usually gentle personalities with the ugly anger they need in war is a way of flattering them into action. |
|---|---|---|
| Instructions | **Answer:** any of 'close the wall up' 'imitate the action' 'Stiffen the sinews' 'summon up the blood' 'Disguise fair nature' | Shakespeare uses the imperative to show Henry commanding his men to be good soldiers. |
| Emotive language | **Answer:** much of the extract is emotive, including 'dear friends', 'English dead', 'modest stillness', 'blast of war' | **Answer:** Shakespeare shows Henry using emotive language to connect with his men and to encourage them to keep fighting. |
| Alliteration | 'blast of war blows in our ears' | **Answer:** The repetition of 'bl' makes a sound a bit like the trumpet calling them to action. |

### Check your skills

Answers will vary as writing and self-assessment will depend on student choices.

## Unit 3: Speaking from experience

*Pages 36–37*

### Activity 1: Word power

a. **1.** spent time with; **2.** assaulted; **3.** turn into a perfect person
b. **1.** that is; **2.** did not; **3.** I am

### Activity 2: Knowledge and understanding

a. Taunting, physical bullying
b. Gratitude, regret, heartbreak

### Activity 3: Reading and understanding

a. Students are likely to agree with statement 2 but not 3 or 1.
b. Sample answer: The final paragraph because it is a combination of current reflections and memories.

### Check your skills

Answers will vary.

## Unit 4: Support our campaign

*Pages 38–39*

### Activity 1: Word power

**a.** Harmful

**b.** Sample answer: careful, beautiful, painful, helpful

### Activity 2: Knowledge and understanding

| | |
|---|---|
| Even some babies have plastic in their blood. | 2 |
| Humans use too much plastic. | 3 |
| Plastic is harmful to animals. | 1 |

### Activity 3: Reading skills

Student responses will vary. Weaker answers may not identify three different phrases nor effectively explain their effect. Stronger answers will explore a range of techniques using accurate terminology.

### Check your skills

1. 'a material that the Earth cannot digest' or 'ingested by wildlife'
2. 'ingested by wildlife' or 'including newborns'
3. 'used for seconds, hours or days, but their remains last forever'

# Chapter 5: Experience and advice

## Unit 1: Adrenaline rush

*Pages 40–41*

### Activity 1: Word power

| Past tense | Present tense |
|---|---|
| The hands <u>bent</u> | The hands <u>bend</u> |
| He <u>tried</u> | He <u>tries</u> |
| A voice <u>shouted</u> | A voice <u>shouts</u> |
| Seth <u>rolled</u> back | Seth <u>rolls</u> back |

### Activity 2: Knowledge and understanding

From the extract:

**a.** Lack of food; Lack of sleep

**b.** Answers may include: 'the shell of a collapsed structure'; 'a place of broken concrete walls'; 'dark shadows'; 'ash-covered pavement'

### Activity 3: Writing skills

Answers are dependent on students' writing choices and will vary. Weaker answers may confuse present and past tense, or start in present tense but lapse into past tense. Stronger answers will include dramatic detail and maintain accurate use of the present tense.

### Check your skills

Answers are dependent on students' writing choices and their self-assessment, and will vary.

## Unit 2: When the soldiers came

*Pages 42–43*

### Activity 1: Knowledge and understanding

True statements:

- Students go to school on buses.
- Malala is used to attention from the media.
- Malala is not afraid to be different from others.

### Activity 2: Reading skills

**a.** Sample answers:

He is a stranger and he can't be seen properly by the girls. The reader begins to feel nervous about what this man may do.

Malala and her friends are used to journalists but the man is not behaving as they expect. This makes them more suspicious.

**b.** Answers may include: All they can see is a small square of sky; The sky they can see is the size of a stamp.

### Check your skills

Grey clouds filled the sky and blocked out the sun. LITERAL

In the sky, silent grey monsters met, waiting to unleash their anger on the world. FIGURATIVE

Answers on effect will vary. Weaker answers may focus on the literal description as it is clear and more accessible. Stronger answers should identify the figurative description as more effective and may explore its use of personification and the way the clouds are given a sinister character.

## Unit 3: Confrontation

*Pages 44–45*

### Activity 1: Word power

Students' responses may vary but a likely order is:

'snapping of tree limbs' 4

'heavy footsteps' 5

'crunching' 2

'low rumbling' 3

'purring noises' 1

### Activity 2: Reading skills

a. A question: 'Maybe the wind had toppled a tree?'
b. A dash: 'I checked the clock – 4 a.m. – and rolled over'
c. Adverbs: 'then', 'really' and 'now'

### Check your skills

Students' responses will vary. Weaker answers will show limited understanding of how to improve the given text. Stronger answers will include questions, dashes and adverbs to help create tension, as well as some sound words (like those from the extract) to build even more tension.

## Unit 4: Advice for Victorian women

*Pages 46–47*

### Activity 1: Word power

Sample answer: 'Delicate' / strong; 'Miserable' / happy; 'Happy' / unhappy

### Activity 2: Knowledge and understanding

Sample answer:
1. Do not make a fine lady of her
2. Let her make tidy her own room.
3. Let her use her hands and her arms.
4. Let her wait upon herself

### Activity 3: Reading skills

Question: Are they happy?
Answer: No, for the want of employment, they are miserable

### Check your skills

Students' written responses will vary and their self-assessment will depend on what they write. Weaker answers may not adapt to the appropriate tone or include the full range of techniques. Stronger answers are likely to manage the imperative tone and to include emotive vocabulary, instructions and rhetorical questions, as well as identify these techniques correctly.

# Chapter 6: Arguments and essays

## Unit 1: Freedom and captivity

*Pages 48–49*

### Activity 1: Knowledge and understanding

These statements are points made in the article:

Circus tigers are probably happier than tigers in zoos. A ban on circus animals is not necessary.

### Activity 2: Writing skills

2. On the other hand, some traditions are worth giving up.
3. However, a law against animals in circuses would help to deal with abusive trainers.
4. And yet, why would we want to teach children to humiliate wild creatures to perform silly tricks?

### Check your skills

Answers will vary depending on student responses. Weaker answers are unlikely to include a full range of arguments and may not sustain a formal tone. Stronger answers will be more accurate, will range across arguments and will manage the correct level of polite formality throughout.

# Unit 2: Reptile alert

*Pages 50–51*

## Activity 1: Knowledge and understanding

a. 'What to consider' and 'Think about'
b. Main heading – What to consider – larger text size and bold
   Subheading – Think about – smaller text size
c. Sample answer: The points have been listed in the order people should think about them. The first things they should think about is whether they can give the pet the right environment. When they have thought about all the other points, they should look at the legal requirements.

## Activity 2: Reading skills

| Nouns | Noun phrases |
|---|---|
| pet | an exotic pet or a realistic pet |
| heating | specialised heating |
| enclosure | size of enclosure |
| paperwork | legal paperwork |

## Check your skills

b. 'burrowing, climbing or basking'
c. 'Our pages on bearded dragons and corn snakes'
d. 'specialist books and leaflets'

# Unit 3: Animal superstar

*Pages 52–53*

## Activity 1: Word power

graceful – clumsy; cleverly – foolishly; attract – repel; feasting – gorging; enjoy – endure; suitable – unsuitable; charming – repulsive

## Activity 2: Writing skills

Student responses will vary. Weaker answers may not sustain a negative tone and may lack subtlety. Stronger answers are likely to make vocabulary choices that indicate a negative attitude and to show feelings through apt choice of details.

## Check your skills

Answers will vary.

# Unit 4: An old warrior

*Pages 54–55*

## Activity 1: Knowledge and understanding

a. He thinks the elephant is valuable.
b. The crowd puts pressure on him.
c. 'a conjurer about to perform a trick'

## Activity 2: Reading skills

Sample answer

| Technique | Example |
|---|---|
| The writer uses repetition to show the pressure he feels from the crowd. | *'glanced round at the crowd'* *'an immense crowd'* |
| The writer uses emotive language to show that the elephant isn't dangerous. | *'peacefully eating'* |
| The writer compares the elephant to important machinery to emphasise its importance. | *'comparable to destroying a huge and costly piece of machinery'* |
| The writer compares the elephant to a cow to show how harmless it is. | *'the elephant looked no more dangerous than a cow'* |

## Check your skills

Students' writing will vary. Weaker answers may not take an advising tone nor a range of arguments. Stronger answers will include modal verbs, emotive language, repetition and comparison.

# Reading

The following assessment criteria are for guidance. It is likely that most students using *Catapult* will attain the Emerging standard or below at the start of secondary school; however, they may show aspects of strength in one of the three attainment objectives, which would take them into the Securing level.

| Oxford Assessment Level | Band | Identify and interpret explicit and implicit information and ideas<br><br>Select and synthesise evidence from within a text and across different texts | Evaluate texts critically and support this with appropriate textual references | Explain, comment on and analyse how writers use language and structure to achieve effects and influence readers, using relevant subject terminology |
|---|---|---|---|---|
| **Extending** | Extending 2 | • Perceptive understanding of texts is demonstrated, with ideas synthesised and evaluated from more than one source, and sophisticated use of reference incorporated to support argument.<br>• Coherent interpretation of texts is developed, based on astute and detailed reading, demonstrating insight. | • Full and perceptive comparison between texts, drawing out similarities and differences in an analytical and critical discussion.<br>• Detailed exploration of how texts are shaped by readers' responses, and well-argued critical and cogent responses to texts. | • Analysis of how specific linguistic, structural and grammatical features are used deliberately to create impact and elicit a particular response in a range of texts.<br>• Confident and integrated use of literary, linguistic and grammatical terminology supporting perceptive and thoughtful critical comments on features in texts. |
| | Extending 1 | • Detailed understanding of texts is demonstrated, with ideas synthesised from more than one source, and precisely selected evidence is used to support and develop arguments.<br>• Interpretations of texts are detailed and based on close and careful reading, developing ideas and drawing out connections. | • Detailed critical comparison between texts, with some analytical explanations.<br>• Exploration of how texts are shaped by readers' responses, and critical opinions are developed, supported by well-argued reasons. | • Some analysis of how linguistic, structural and grammatical features are used in a range of texts to create specific effects.<br>• Confident use of a range of literary, linguistic and grammatical terminology, supporting critical and analytical commentary on texts. |
| **Securing** | Securing 3 | • Clear understanding of the difference between main and subsidiary ideas is demonstrated, with some ability to summarise and synthesise information, supported by well-selected evidence.<br>• Inferences develop an interpretation of texts, exploring ideas and beginning to make connections. | • Critical comparisons between texts, including some ability to contrast ideas, with explanations of comments.<br>• Discussion of how texts are shaped by readers' responses and critical, personal opinions are developed, supported by sound reasons. | • Detailed exploration of how a variety of linguistic, structural and grammatical features are used in a range of texts.<br>• Mostly confident use of literary, linguistic and grammatical terminology, helping to support detailed and critical commentary on texts. |

| Oxford Assessment Level | Band | Identify and interpret explicit and implicit information and ideas<br><br>Select and synthesise evidence from within a text and across different texts | Evaluate texts critically and support this with appropriate textual references | Explain, comment on and analyse how writers use language and structure to achieve effects and influence readers, using relevant subject terminology |
|---|---|---|---|---|
| **Securing** | Securing 2 | • Main ideas and subsidiary ideas are understood and summarised in a range of texts, with well-selected evidence used to support arguments.<br>• Inferences across a text or texts, beginning to explore layers of meaning. | • Critical comparisons are made between texts, with some explanation of comments.<br>• Some exploration of the effect of texts on different readers, with developed personal and critical opinions offered. | • Some exploration of how different linguistic, structural and grammatical features are used in a range of texts.<br>• Use of appropriate literary, linguistic and grammatical terminology helps support effective commentary on texts. |
| | Securing 1 | • Understanding of the difference between main and subsidiary points in a range of texts is shown, with appropriate evidence used to expand ideas.<br>• Inferences across a text, or texts, begin to show some evidence of development and exploration. | • Some critical comparisons made between texts, with some development of comments.<br>• Some consideration of the effects of texts on readers, and personal, critical opinions show evidence of some development. | • Some discussion of how linguistic, structural and grammatical features are used in different texts.<br>• Secure knowledge of terminology to support explanation of literary, linguistic and grammatical features in texts. |
| **Developing** | Developing 2 | • Clear understanding of explicit meaning is shown, with main points of some texts summarised, and relevant evidence used to support ideas.<br>• Inferences based on evidence across a text, with some development. | • Comparisons are made between texts, with some expansion of comments.<br>• Understanding of the effect of texts on the reader is shown, and personal opinions are justified with straightforward reasons. | • Some explanation of aspects of language and structure, including grammatical features.<br>• Developing knowledge of some of the relevant terminology to discuss literary, linguistic and grammatical features in texts is shown. |
| | Developing 1 | • Straightforward understanding of explicit meaning, main ideas are identified and some evidence is used to support ideas.<br>• Inferences based on evidence from different points in a text, with some explanation. | • Straightforward comparison is made between texts, with limited development of comments.<br>• Understanding of effect of the text on reader is shown and straightforward personal opinions given. | • Some straightforward aspects of language and structure are identified, including grammatical features.<br>• Familiarity with some appropriate terminology to discuss literary, grammatical and linguistic features in texts. |
| **Emerging** | Emerging 2 | • Some understanding of explicit meaning, key details and less familiar information are identified from longer sections of text.<br>• Inferences based on evidence from the text, with limited explanation. | • Some appropriate comparisons made between texts, but comments aren't necessarily developed.<br>• Appreciation of effect of the text on reader is shown and personal opinions expressed. | • Some straightforward aspects of language and structure are identified, including more familiar grammatical features.<br>• Some use of appropriate terminology to discuss more familiar literary, grammatical and linguistic features in texts, with some limited discussion of these features. |
| | Emerging 1 | • Some understanding of explicit meaning, familiar information and key details are identified when guidance is given on location.<br>• Basic inferences made, although these aren't always linked to evidence from the text. | • Attempts to make comparisons between texts, but these are not always relevant.<br>• Personal opinions about the text expressed, but limited appreciation of the effect of the text on other readers. | • Identification of straightforward aspects of language and structure, including grammatical features, is attempted but not always successfully.<br>• Occasional use of appropriate terminology to identify more familiar literary, grammatical and linguistic features in texts. |

# Writing

The following assessment criteria are for guidance. It is likely that most students using *Catapult* will attain the Emerging standard or below at the start of secondary school; however, they may show aspects of strength in one of the three attainment objectives (Form and Structure, Style and Vocabulary, Grammatical range and accuracy), which would take them into the Securing level. Similarly, some students might have severe weaknesses spelling or punctuation while still showing secure awareness of form and structure.

| Oxford Assessment Level | Band | Form and structure | Style and vocabulary | Grammatical range and accuracy |
|---|---|---|---|---|
| **Extending** | Extending 2 | • Imaginative and skilful adaptation of form used to address a range of purposes and create impact on the reader, across a range of texts<br>• Structure and organisational devices are deployed flexibly and adroitly to fulfil the purpose of the writing and position the reader | • Style draws on a range of techniques and is nuanced to be appropriate to purpose and audience, and to meet the requirements of a task.<br>• Use of vocabulary is ambitious, judicious and sometimes deliberately surprising. | • Varied syntax is used in a range of writing to convey ideas and create impact for the reader.<br>• A range of punctuation is used with precision and accuracy to create effects; errors are rare or untypical.<br>• Spelling is correct, with errors untypical or evident only in very unusual words. |
| | Extending 1 | • Across a range of texts, form is adapted to meet the purpose of the writing, drawing on a range of conventions.<br>• Information and ideas are skilfully controlled and organised, with a range of devices used to position the reader. | • A range of stylistic features within a deliberately chosen style are used to create particular impact for purpose and audience.<br>• A wide, ambitious and imaginative vocabulary is used across a range of texts with precision. | • Syntax is varied and apposite, showing an ability to adapt features for particular forms of writing.<br>• A range of punctuation is used with precision and accuracy to create effects: there may be one-off errors in more complex sentences<br>• Spelling is correct with only occasional errors in irregular or unusual words. |
| **Securing** | Securing 3 | • The form is adapted to suit the purpose of the writing, showing familiarity with a range of conventions.<br>• The structure is controlled, with paragraphs used to position the reader. | • Consistent use of a range of styles, including formal and informal, appropriate to purpose and audience.<br>• Vocabulary chosen is varied and ambitious, and selected to fulfil the purpose of a task. | • Syntax is used with some skill to create particular effects.<br>• A range of punctuation is used with precision and accuracy to create effects; there may be some errors in more complex sentences.<br>• Spelling is almost always correct, though there may be errors in some less common, irregular or commonly misspelled words. |
| | Securing 2 | • There is some adaptation of form, appropriate to purpose and audience, in some texts.<br>• A clear structure and a variety of paragraphs are used to support the purpose of the writing | • The chosen style is mostly sustained throughout the writing, appropriate to purpose, audience and level of formality.<br>• A wide vocabulary, including some ambitious words, is used appropriate to the purpose of a task. | • Sentence structures are chosen and adapted to meet the requirements of the task.<br>• A range of punctuation is used for clarity and impact, with only occasional omissions or errors.<br>• Spelling is mostly correct, though there may be occasional errors in less common, irregular words. |
| | Securing 1 | • Use of form shows secure understanding of purpose and audience across a range of texts.<br>• The structure of the writing is clear, with connectives used to signal the sequence of ideas in the text and secure use of paragraphing. | • A range of stylistic features, including those appropriate for formal writing, used to support the purpose of the writing.<br>• A range of vocabulary is used, including technical, literary and subject specific language, to match purpose and style, and sometimes for particular effect. | • A range of sentence structures is used, almost always securely, with some adaptation to the purpose of the task.<br>• A range of punctuation is used, mostly securely, to clarify meaning and sometimes for effect.<br>• Most spelling is correct including less common, irregular words. |

| Oxford Assessment Level | Band | Form and structure | Style and vocabulary | Grammatical range and accuracy |
|---|---|---|---|---|
| **Developing** | Developing 2 | • The main features of a form are used, mostly securely, showing understanding of purpose and audience.<br>• The overall structure of the writing is clear, supported by appropriate use of paragraphs | • Some range of stylistic features is used, mostly appropriately, to support the purpose of the writing.<br>• Vocabulary is selected to match the purpose and style of writing, mostly appropriately, including some technical and literary language. | • A range of sentence structures, simple, co-ordinated and complex, are used, mostly securely, though there may be occasional errors.<br>• Some range of punctuation is used, mostly securely, to achieve clarity in texts.<br>• Most spelling is correct, including common irregular words and some less common words. |
| | Developing 1 | • The main features of a form are used, showing understanding of purpose and some awareness of audience, though not always sustained throughout.<br>• Writing has straightforward overall structure, with mostly secure use of sections or paragraphs. | • Some stylistic features are used, mostly appropriately, to match the purpose of the writing.<br>• Some range of vocabulary is used, mostly appropriately, for purpose and audience | • Some range of sentence structures is used, mostly accurately, though there may be a lack of variety or some lack of control when more ambitious structures are attempted.<br>• Punctuation of sentences is mostly accurate, with some use of other punctuation, e.g. commas and apostrophes for omission.<br>• Spelling of most regularly constructed words and common irregular words is accurate. |
| **Emerging** | Emerging 2 | • The main features of a form are used, demonstrating some understanding of purpose and basic awareness of audience, though the use of these features is not always successful.<br>• Writing has a simple structure, with the use of sections and paragraphs beginning to be secured. | • Some stylistic features are used to match the purpose of the writing, although these are not always employed successfully.<br>• Beginning to use a range of vocabulary, although this isn't always employed successfully. | • Some range of sentence structures is used, though there may be lapses in accuracy when more ambitious structures are attempted.<br>• Punctuation of sentences is often accurate, but the use of other punctuation, e.g. commas and apostrophes for omission, is limited.<br>• Spelling of most regularly constructed words and common irregular words is mostly accurate. |
| | Emerging 1 | • Some attempts made to use the main features of a form, demonstrating limited awareness of purpose and audience.<br>• Writing has a basic structure, supported by the occasional use of sections and paragraphs. | • Occasional use of stylistic features, although these are not always employed successfully.<br>• Attempts to use a range of vocabulary, with some limited success. | • Limited range of sentence structures is used, with lapses in accuracy when multi-clause structures are attempted.<br>• Punctuation of sentences is sometimes accurate, but with lapses in the use of other punctuation, e.g. comma splicing. Spelling of most regularly constructed words is sometimes accurate. |

# KS3 National Curriculum and *Catapult* matching chart: Reading

| National Curriculum: subject content | Chapter 1: Character and setting | Chapter 2: Action and atmosphere | Chapter 3: Explanations and insights | Chapter 4: Opinion and persuasion | Chapter 5: Experience and advice | Chapter 6: Arguments and essays |
|---|---|---|---|---|---|---|
| Reading a wide range of fiction and non-fiction, including in particular whole books, short stories, poems and plays with a wide coverage of genres, historical periods, forms and authors. The range will include high-quality works from: (R1a) | SB: U1, U2, U3, U4, U5<br>WB: U1, U2, U3, U4, U5 | SB: U1, U2, U3, U4, U5<br>WB: U1, U2, U3, U4, U5 | SB: U1, U2, U3, U4<br>WB: U1, U2, U3, U4 | SB: U1, U2, U3, U4<br>WB: U1, U2, U3, U4 | SB: U1, U2, U3, U4<br>WB: U1, U2, U3, U4 | SB: U1, U2, U3, U4<br>WB: U1, U2, U3, U4 |
| • English literature, both pre-1914 and contemporary, including prose, poetry and drama (R1a1) | SB: U1, U2, U3, U4, U5<br>WB: U1, U2, U3, U4, U5 | SB: U1, U2, U3, U4, U5<br>WB: U1, U2, U3, U4, U5 | | | WB: U1 | SB: U1 |
| • Shakespeare (two plays) (R1a2) | | | | WB: U2 | | |
| • seminal world literature (R1a3) | | | | | | |
| Choosing and reading books independently for challenge, interest and enjoyment (R1b) | | | | | | |
| Re-reading books encountered earlier to increase familiarity with them and provide a basis for making comparisons (R1c) | SB: U4, U5<br>WB: U4, U5 | | SB: U1<br>WB: U1 | | | |
| Learning new vocabulary, relating it explicitly to known vocabulary and understanding it with the help of context and dictionaries (R2a) | SB: U1, U2, U3, U4, U5<br>WB: U1 | SB: U1, U2, U3, U4, U5<br>WB: U1, U2, U4, U5 | SB: U1, U2, U3, U4<br>WB: U2, U4 | SB: U1, U2, U3, U4<br>WB: U1, U3, U4 | SB: U1, U2, U3, U4<br>WB: U1, U3, U4 | SB: U1, U2, U3, U4<br>WB: U3 |
| Making inferences and referring to evidence in the text (R2b) | SB: U2, U3, U4, U5<br>WB: U2, U3, U4, U5 | SB: U5<br>WB: U5 | | SB: U4 | SB: U2<br>WB: U2 | |
| Knowing the purpose, audience for and context of the writing and drawing on this knowledge to support comprehension (R2c) | SB: U1, U2, U3, U4, U5 | SB: U1, U2, U3, U4, U5 | SB: U1, U2, U3, U4<br>WB: U1, U3 | SB: U1, U2, U3, U4<br>WB: U1, U2, U3 | SB: U1, U2, U3, U4 | SB: U1, U2, U3, U4<br>WB: U2 |
| Checking their understanding to make sure that what they have read makes sense (R2d) | SB: U1, U2, U3, U4, U5<br>WB: U1, U2, U3, U4, U5 | SB: U1, U2, U3, U4, U5<br>WB: U3, U4 | SB: U1, U2, U3, U4<br>WB: U1, U2, U3 | SB: U1, U2, U3, U4<br>WB: U2, U3, U4 | SB: U1, U2, U3, U4<br>WB: U1, U2, U4 | SB: U1, U2, U3, U4<br>WB: U1, U2, U4 |
| Knowing how language, including figurative language, vocabulary choice, grammar, text structure and organisational features, presents meaning (R3a) | SB: U1, U2, U3, U5<br>WB: U1, U3, U4 | SB: U1, U2, U3, U4, U5<br>WB: U1, U2, U3, U4 | SB: U1, U2, U3, U4<br>WB: U1, U3, U4 | SB: U1, U2, U3, U4<br>WB: U1, U2, U3, U4 | SB: U1, U2, U3, U4<br>WB: U1, U2, U3, U4 | SB: U1, U2, U3, U4<br>WB: U2, U4 |

| National Curriculum: subject content | Chapter 1: Character and setting | Chapter 2: Action and atmosphere | Chapter 3: Explanations and insights | Chapter 4: Opinion and persuasion | Chapter 5: Experience and advice | Chapter 6: Arguments and essays |
|---|---|---|---|---|---|---|
| Recognising a range of poetic conventions and understanding how these have been used (R3b) | SB: U3<br>WB: U3 | | | | | SB: U1 |
| Studying setting, plot and characterisation, and the effects of these (R3c) | SB: U1, U2, U4, U5<br>WB: U1, U4, U5 | WB: U2, U3, U5<br>WB: U2, U3 | SB: U2<br>WB: U1 | | | |
| Understanding how the work of dramatists is communicated effectively through performance and how alternative staging allows for different interpretations of a play (R3d) | | | | | | |
| Making critical comparisons across texts (R3e) | | | | | | |
| Studying a range of authors, including at least two authors in depth each year (R3f) | SB: U1, U2, U3, U4, U5<br>WB: U1, U2, U3, U4, U5 | SB: U1, U2, U3, U4, U5<br>WB: U1, U2, U3, U4, U5 | SB: U1, U2, U3, U4<br>WB: U1, U2, U3, U4 | SB: U1, U2, U3, U4<br>WB: U1, U2, U3, U4 | SB: U1, U2, U3, U4<br>WB: U1, U2, U3, U4 | SB: U1, U2, U3, U4<br>WB: U1, U2, U3, U4 |

SB = Student Book
WB = Workbook
U = Unit

Please note: some of the higher-order skills not covered in *Catapult English Student Book 1* and *Workbook 1* will be covered in *Catapult* English 2.

# KS3 National Curriculum and *Catapult* matching chart: Writing

| National Curriculum: subject content | Chapter 1: Character and setting | Chapter 2: Action and atmosphere | Chapter 3: Explanations and insights | Chapter 4: Opinion and persuasion | Chapter 5: Experience and advice | Chapter 6: Arguments and essays |
|---|---|---|---|---|---|---|
| Writing for a wide range of purposes and audiences, including: (W1a) | | | SB: U4 | SB: U2, U4 | | SB: U1 |
| • well-structured formal expository and narrative essays (W1a1) | SB: U1, U2 | SB: U1, U2, U3, U4 WB: U1, U2, U3, U5 | SB: U3 | WB: U3 | SB: U1, U3 WB: U1 | SB: U3 |
| • stories, scripts, poetry and other imaginative writing (W1a2) | | | | SB: U1 WB: U2 | | |
| • notes and polished scripts for talks and presentations (W1a3) | SB: U1, U3, U4, U5 WB: U5 | | SB: U1, U2, U3 WB: U1, U2, U3 | SB: U3 | SB: U4 WB: U4 | WB: U1, U3 |
| • a range of other narrative and non-narrative texts, including arguments, and personal and formal letters (W1a4) | | | SB: U1, U2, U3, U4 WB: U1, U2 | SB: U1, U3, U4 WB: U2 | SB: U1, U4 WB: U4 | SB: U1. U3 WB: U1, U3 |
| Applying their growing knowledge of vocabulary, grammar and text structure to their writing and selecting the appropriate form (W1c) | SB: U1, U2, U3, U4, U5 | SB: U1, U2, U3, U4, U5 WB: U2, U3, U5 | SB: U1, U2, U3, U4 WB: U3 | SB: U1, U2, U3 WB: U2, U3 | SB: U1, U2, U3, U4 WB: U1, U3, U4 | SB: U1, U2, U3 WB: U1 |
| Drawing on knowledge of literary and rhetorical devices from their reading and listening to enhance the impact of their writing (W1d) | SB: U5 | SB: U1, U3, U5 WB: U1, U3, U5 | SB: U3 WB: U3 | SB: U1, U3 WB: U2, U3 | SB: U3, U4 WB: U3, U4 | |
| Considering how their writing reflects the audiences and purposes for which it was intended (W2a) | | SB: U1 WB: U5 | SB: U1, U3 WB: U3 | SB: U1, U3 | | |
| Amending the vocabulary, grammar and structure of their writing to improve its coherence and overall effectiveness (W2b) | | SB: U2 WB: U2 | | | WB: U1 | |
| Paying attention to accurate grammar, punctuation and spelling; applying the spelling patterns and rules set out in English Appendix 1 to the Key Stage 1 and 2 programmes of study for English (W2c) | SB: U1, U2, U3, U4, U5 WB: U5 | SB: U1, U2, U3, U4 WB: U1, U2, U3, U5 | SB: U1, U2, U3, U4 WB: U1, U2, U3 | SB: U1, U2, U3, U4 WB: U2, U3, U4 | SB: U1, U3, U4 WB: U1, U4 | SB: U1, U3 WB: U1, U3 |

SB = Student Book
WB = Workbook
U = Unit

# KS3 National Curriculum and *Catapult* matching chart: Grammar and vocabulary

| National Curriculum: subject content | Chapter 1: Character and setting | Chapter 2: Action and atmosphere | Chapter 3: Explanations and insights | Chapter 4: Opinion and persuasion | Chapter 5: Experience and advice | Chapter 6: Arguments and essays |
|---|---|---|---|---|---|---|
| Extending and applying the grammatical knowledge set out in English Appendix 2 to the Key Stage 1 and 2 programmes of study to analyse more challenging texts (G1) | SB: U1, U2, U3 WB: U1 | SB: U1, U2 WB: U1, U2, U4, U5 | SB: U3, U4 WB: U3, U4 | SB: U1, U3, U4 WB: U1, U2, U3 | SB: U1, U3, U4 WB: U3 | SB: U1, U2, U4 WB: U4 |
| Studying the effectiveness and impact of the grammatical features of the texts they read (G2) | SB: U2, U3 WB: U2 | SB: U1, U2, U5 WB: U2, U5 | SB: U1, U3, U4 WB: U3, U4 | SB: U1, U2, U3, U4 WB: U1, U2, U3, U4 | SB: U1, U3, U4 WB: U1, U3, U4 | SB: U1, U2, U3, U4 WB: U2, U4 |
| Drawing on new vocabulary and grammatical constructions from their reading and listening, and using these consciously in their writing and speech to achieve particular effects (G3) | SB: U1, U2, U3, U4, U5 | SB: U1, U2, U3, U5 WB: U2, U5 | SB: U1, U3 WB: U1, U3, U4 | WB: U1, U3 WB: U2, U3 | SB: U1, U3, U4 WB: U1, U3, U4 | SB: U1, U2, U3 WB: U4 |
| Knowing and understanding the differences between spoken and written language, including differences associated with formal and informal registers, and between Standard English and other varieties of English (G4) | | | | SB: U1, U2 WB: U1, U2, U3 | | |
| Using Standard English confidently in their own writing and speech (G5) | SB: U2 WB: U2 | SB: U1, U2, U3, U5 WB: U1, U2, U3, U5 | SB: U1, U3 WB: U1, U3 | SB: U1, U3 WB: U1, U3 | SB: U1, U3 WB: U1, U3 | SB: U1, U3 WB: U1, U3, U4 |
| Discussing reading, writing and spoken language with precise and confident use of linguistic and literary terminology (G6) | SB: U3, U5 | SB: U4 | SB: U4 | SB: U2, U4 WB: U1 | SB: U2 WB: U2 | SB: U2, U4 |

SB = Student Book
WB = Workbook
U = Unit

# *Catapult* Student Book 1: Key terms glossary

**adjective** a word that describes a person, place or object

**adverb** a word that gives more detail about a verb, an adjective or another adverb

**alliteration** using the same letter or sound at the beginning of several words for special effect

**anecdote** a short story about a real person or event

**atmosphere** the feeling or mood given by the writing, often linked to the setting or situation

**autobiography** the story of a person's life, written by that person

**biography** the story of a person's life, written by someone else

**chronicle** chain of historical events

**clause** a group of words with a verb

**conclusion** ending

**conjunction** a linking word, also known as a 'connective', that joins words or groups of words together, e.g. if, but or and

**context** the parts of a text that come immediately before and after a word and clarify its meaning, or the background against which something happens

**contrast** to compare two things to show their differences

**dash** a punctuation mark (–) used to show a pause

**dialogue** the words spoken by characters in a play, film or story

**expository essay** an essay in which a writer explores different ideas about a subject, weighing up the evidence for and against these and setting out their own point of view

**extended metaphor** a lengthy description that describes something as something else in order to create a vivid picture in the reader's mind

**fiction** writing, such as stories, which describes imaginary events or people

**figurative language** words or expressions with a meaning that is different from the literal meaning

**flashback** a story technique that takes the reader back in time to events that happened before the main story

**imagery** writing that creates a picture in the reader's mind or appeals to other senses

**imply** suggest something without saying it directly

**infer** work something out from what is seen, said or done, even though it is not stated directly

**inference** a sensible suggestion of what is meant, based on clues given in the text

**main clause** a clause that contains a subject and verb, and makes sense on its own

**metaphor** describing something as something else, not meant to be taken literally, e.g. 'You are a star'

**modal verb** a type of verb that shows possibility or likelihood, e.g. *can, could, may, might, should*

**multi-clause sentence** a sentence made up of more than one clause, each with its own verb

**narrative essay** an essay that focuses on the writer's personal experience

**narrator** the person who tells the story

**non-fiction** writing that is informative or factual

**noun** a word used to name a place, person, feeling, thing or idea

**noun phrase** a group of words that has a noun as its head or key word. All the words in the group tell us more about the head noun, e.g. *a big muddy puddle* ('puddle' is the head noun)

**novel** a story which shows characters and action in a realistic way

**passive voice** when the subject of the sentence is acted on by the verb, e.g. *The window had been broken by the burglar*

**past tense** used to describe things that have already happened

**personification** representing an idea in human form or a thing as having human characteristics

**phrase** a group of words that form a unit

**poetic language** language that uses vocabulary, images and forms often found in poems

**prefix** a word or group of letters placed in front of another word to add to or change its meaning

**present tense** used to describe things that are happening now

**pronoun** a word that can be used instead of a noun, e.g. *she, it, his*

**rhetorical question** a question asked for dramatic effect and not intended to get an answer

**rhyming couplet** lines of verse next to each other that rhyme; they are usually the same length

**rhythm** the pattern made by the 'beats' in language or music

**second-person narrative** written from the point of view of the narrator telling the story to a character, using 'you' and 'yours'. It is as if the reader is another character in the story

**second-person pronoun** you, your or yours

**sentence structure** how a sentence is put together, including word and punctuation choices and word order

**setting** the time and place where the action of a story happens

**simile** a comparison that uses the word 'like' or 'as', e.g. *as cold as ice*

**stanza** a verse of poetry

**structure** how a text is ordered, the connections made between ideas and themes, and where the writer is directing the reader's focus

**subheading** a title given to a section of text

**summary** a short text giving just the main points

**suspense** an anxious or uncertain feeling while waiting for something to happen or become known

**symbol** something that stands for or represents something else

**synonym** a word that means the same or almost the same as another word, e.g. 'glad' is a synonym for 'happy'

**tone** the way a writer expresses his or her attitude to the subject

**verb** a word that identifies actions, thoughts, feelings or a state of being

**verb tenses** the three main verb tenses are past tense, present tense and future tense; each one tells you when something happened